JOSE PAULO DOS SANTOS

CONTEMPORARY
WORLD
ARCHITECTS

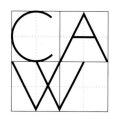

JOSE PAULO DOS SANTOS

Compiled by
Oscar Riera Ojeda

Introduction by
Gerrit Confurius

Concept and Design by
Lucas H. Guerra
Oscar Riera Ojeda

ROCKPORT PUBLISHERS
GLOUCESTER, MASSACHUSETTS

First published in the United States of America by:
Rockport Publishers, Inc.
33 Commercial Street
Gloucester, Massachusetts 01930
Telephone: 978-282-9590
Fax: 978-283-2742
www.rockpub.com

Other distribution by Rockport Publishers, Inc.

ISBN 1-56496-573-2
10 9 8 7 6 5 4 3 2 1
Manufactured in China

Cover photograph: Kindertagesstätte by Christian Richters
Back cover photographs: (Top) House in Pego, and (Bottom) Loios Convent
Renovation and Extension by Luis Ferreira Alves
Back flap photograph: Jose Paulo dos Santos by Luis Ferreira Alves
Pages 1–3 photograph: Loios Convent Renovation and Extension by Luis Ferreira Alves
Page 143 photograph: Office Portrait by Luis Ferreira Alves

Graphic Design: Lucas H. Guerra/Oscar Riera Ojeda
Layout: Oscar Riera Ojeda
Composition: Garrick Jones

CONTENTS

Introduction

BY GERRIT CONFURIUS

THE ARCHITECT'S CRAFT

Unlike many other contemporary architects, whose ambition it is to distinguish themselves with a unique signature, José Paulo dos Santos' work is imbued with a more anonymous elegance. His architecture is never the celebration of his own skill, never draws attention to himself as a person. Rather, his own role in its creation disappears in the astonishing self-evidence of the best solution; a lesson in austerity, it opposes any kind of rhetorical self-glorification and confirms the architect's status as a good craftsman. An idea originally applied to Adolf Loos holds true for dos Santos as well: To be silent, where you cannot speak, to do nothing but construct a technically correct building in a proper human demeanor, from which the only right and truly modern form will result of its own accord. The form should not be intentionally applied to the building or object of use by the architect; rather, it should manifest itself in it. A kind of modernity, that doesn't say: look here, how modern I am.

The best introduction to dos Santos' formal world is the Pousada de Nossa Senhora da Assunção near Arraiolos. The former monastery, not far from Evora on a slope at the foot of the Arraiolos mountains below a fortress, was originally founded by the Loios Order as a hospital under the patronage of a wealthy aristocrat who had returned from India. The cornerstone was laid in 1527. Twenty years ago, the property was acquired by the state, and in 1993 was selected for participation in a state program in support of architecture and tourism, the revival of an initiative begun under Salazar in the 1940s, when selected architects were commissioned to build hotels along the main routes. The list of these Pousadas—now primarily renovations of historic buildings—reads like a "Who's who" of contemporary Portuguese architecture. And so it happened that the near-ruined convent now gleams in the almost painfully bright whitewash common in Alentejo, where extensive areas are farmed in monoculture and buildings appear here and there, on the tops of small hills.

The renovation of the Pousada Nossa Senhora da Assunção consisted of the reconstruction and restoration of the church—with new pews, pulpit, and table in a simplified form reminiscent of the reductionism of Dom van der Laan—as well as the remodeling of the agricultural buildings and other structures. Agricultural activities on the sizeable grounds were also revitalized with the planting of olive trees, orange trees, and grapevines and the restoration of the cloister gardens and fountains. The core of the work is the restoration and expansion of the monastery. Here, many functions received a new space and many spaces a new function within the generously expanded facilities.

The new program required an additional wing and several expansions, which the architect incorporated into a double-courtyard complex. The new patio, twice as big as the old one, preserves the original proportions; nearly quadratic in form, it intensifies and enlarges the experience of the old, open courtyard without upstaging its modest monumentality, without any kind of "emotional athletics" (Loos). In the addition of a new wing on the east side of the patio the horizontal predominates as strongly as with da Graca, or even Dudok. The emphatic horizontality of the new wing is underscored by the window openings, which stand in clear contrast to the historical part of the complex with its emphasis on the vertical in windows and pinnacles. On the interior, the new building accommodates guest rooms arranged in a single row and the functional organization of new service spaces.

Though unabashedly modern in many of its parts, the new wing appears to have been added organically. No attempts were made to hide the boundary, the rupture; yet the whole appears as if there had never been a break. The modernist idiosyncrasy of pressing for innovation without being able to renounce or discard anything is thus pleasantly tempered and civilized. It is the most distant possible approach to a time in which tradition still lived, when the self-awareness and guilt of the modern age had not yet awakened and the past had not yet been sentimentalized and archived as something irretrievably lost. The elegance of the addition causes the old, whether restored or altered, to appear well-preserved and well-tended; both the old and the modern appear timeless and thus familiar with each other. As Loos put it: "You can best tell whether a thing is modern by whether or not it is at home in the company of old things." The new building is characterized by sharp geometric articulation and extreme precision in the use of building materials—as sharp-edged and white as if sawn out by a machine, as smoothly plastered and accurately cut as if faced with a metal plate—qualities that rub off on the old structure as well. The whole is reminiscent of Venturi's "Complexity and Contradiction": as a rule, historical buildings and cities, the result of long processes of development, do not show stylistic unity and formal agreement among their parts. Yet the heterogeneous parts still combine to form a whole, and all the more so, the more visible the discrepancies and ruptures are allowed to remain.

Marcel Proust once said of the old palaces of the nobility that there remained "an excess of luxury, no longer truly usable in a modern hotel, which now, devoid of any practical value, took on a life of its own in its futility." He doubted whether the bourgeoisie who moved into these old palaces as residents or hotel guests could adequately dignify or fill them. Yet the quality of the place is grounded to a not inconsiderable extent in precisely this inadequacy, this strangeness, the discrepancy of role and freedom of projection. This "life of its own"—the involuntary exaggeration, undeserved dignity, borrowed elegance, wasted luxury—is a source of pleasure and character.

In accord with the rules of modernist practice, the interior is newly articulated to reflect functional differentiation and arranged into sequences through patterns of circulation. The new program constitutes a loose interpretation of the original function, resulting in interesting "misunderstandings." As the architect himself felicitously expressed it, the whole is characterized by "functional clarity in labyrinthine disguise." Indeed, there are many similarities between cloister and hotel, many of the same rituals. The monks' cells and agricultural pursuits, a life rooted in the landscape with its rituals, has yielded to the leisure of the tourists, whose rituals find an eminently suitable and luxurious frame in this monastic setting and infrastructure. Secluded hotels in the country, with their own agriculture, sports facilities, and church, suggest the comparison to a particular extent. They also share what Roland Barthes describes as the attempt "to bind happiness to a finite and organized space," to invent a kind of self-sufficient boarding school. Like the cloister, the hotel is marked by an intensified organization of daily life; it has an established schedule, its own kitchen, a dress code, personnel, guardians of the rules, and prescribed modes of communication, but also special pleasures, physical training, leisure, luxury, the pleasant relief from absolute self-determination, the opportunity to surrender to a prescribed order. A pleasant discipline is imposed upon life. The carefully devised arrangement of rooms corresponds to this regimen, with spaces reserved for particular moments and pleasures.

(above left) Loios Convent: overview showing the added wing, right foreground, with the new service area below the east-facing terrace; (above right) Detail of a new frame set in the existing wall, minimizing its external massing.

As in the monastery, much is intended to prevent boredom, which gives rise to sinful thoughts. A certain degree of de-individualization appears to be the condition for architecture in an emotional sense.

The buildings are social models, reduced versions of a utopia patterned after Phalanstère or Versailles. Indeed, in its very idea—in accord with an unattainable but effectual ideal—a hotel is a laboratory for Fourier's "new order of love." The magic arises from a secret understanding among those present, who submitted themselves to a strange law when they entered the building: availability for happiness. Already as a young man growing up in a hotel, Jose Paulo learned how architecture can effortlessly harmonize with the pleasures of life and the easy fellowship of guests strange to one another, what elevates a person in the service of a patient intensification of the feeling of aliveness, and how much discipline and order this relaxation requires.

Like the church and the cloister, the hotel is a sanctuary of silence. As Thomas Mann described it in Death in Venice: "The room was suffused with the solemn stillness that belongs to the ambition of great hotels. The waiters went about on padded soles. The rattling of a teapot, a half-whispered word was all that could be heard." In dos Santos' Pousada, stillness is associated with timelessness and indeterminate age, especially of the new courtyard. The differently shaped chimneys, towers, simplified portals, lemon trees, water basin, and the mute wall of the new building with its slit and low-seeming driveway—all these elements are incorporated into a comprehensive dramaturgy that shows the things, familiar in and of themselves, in an unusual constellation, as if they did not or no longer fit with each other. Time stands still, as if at a turning point. Nietzsche described this condition as "quiet at midday": "Whoever has been apportioned an active morning of life, at life's midday his soul is overcome by a strange yearning for quiet.... It grows still around him, the voices sound further and further away; the sun shines down on him from above." He lies in a wooded glade and "it seems to him that all the things of nature have fallen asleep with him, the expression of eternity in their faces. He wants nothing... his heart stands still, only his eye lives—it is a death with open eyes. There he sees much that he never saw before, and as far as he sees, everything is spun into a net of light, as if buried in it.... Then at last the wind rises in the trees, the midday is past, and life seizes him again, the life with blind eyes." In that interval, things appear as if in a still life. The unquiet of the world, to which it owes all work, is forgotten for a moment, and with it the occasional sense of the meaninglessness of the eternal cycle. This "aesthetic condition," relieved of the driving will, "is the painless condition" the Greeks also praised as the condition of the gods. "In that moment we are exempt from the base urge of the will; we celebrate a Sabbath from the prison of desire...." The things are waiting for something. They exude an atmosphere of the "metaphysical," as Di Chirico described it, or of pensiveness, as Nietzsche would have said.

The special intensity of the images, however, arises from the stillness that pervades them. It is not only the stillness that remains when the noise ceases at midday; it is not a dependent, temporary stillness, but one that fills the space, dominates it, occupies it, a stillness that is in fact identical with the space. In these spaces, one can move in any direction, with no hurry. There is an infinite amount of time for everything; nothing is urgent. The stillness is like another state of being, in which everything pauses, waiting until you are ready. Here the

(previous page) Various additions to
the Convent's agricultural wing, which
had initially been used as a cattle shed:
(left) the director's flat; (middle) the
service zone for staff and the kitchen;
(right) a disguised tower for the new
elevator shaft in the newly enclosed
patio. (this page) A reflecting pool medi-
ates the area between sleeping rooms
and the restaurant, from the newly
enclosed patio to the eastern terrace.

"knower" is in his element; but the "man without qualities" would feel at home too. Here no one accuses him of indecision or passivity; those who would are barred from this condition. Here, nothing is more important than anything else; everything is equally possible. The condition is like the man himself, "equally near and equally distant to all the qualities" of his own person.

In the convent, the paths leave the impression that they could always be trod in the opposite direction as well. The circulation system is invested with a special organizing power. The whole is not a series of spaces with differing purposes or functions, but is conceived architecturally as an endless promenade embracing both interior and exterior, a system of frames and terminations, an endless series of surprises. Stairs and hallways are interrupted again and again by pedestals, views, windows with seats in the form of rounded stone slabs. All of these elements are part of the design, as is the variation in ceiling heights. In the breakfast room, the windows to the courtyard are at floor level. The men's room is a cell of large granite squares, with one omitted for a window at floor level. The refectory is connected to the cloister through windows that extend to the ground like doors, and could even be used as such. There are doors that are surprisingly small, just as there are windows that are surprisingly large.

The passage from the second large courtyard to the esplanade with the swimming pool is an extraordinary physical experience, one of diving under and emerging from the closed, white new wing through a low-hung opening, made optically narrower—but also softened—by the gray of the granite under the white skin.

From the breakfast room, a round-arched door leads back to the encircling passages; like a revolving door, it sits at the lowest and narrowest point of a series of successively narrower vaults, of ever lower arches, slightly twisted as if into a snail's shell. It recalls the rotating wheel of an intake pump, ensuring the consistency of the water flow. This system of hallways, passages, transitions, and points of interest stands in relation to the view seen on the outside: the slight incline of the hill, the gently sloping terrain, and to the northeast the open landscape, as far as the eye can see. In the breakfast room, heating and ventilation units are positioned before the piers in granite escarpments; elsewhere, they are set into the floor. Toward the courtyard, the cloister is enclosed with glass—glass boxes framed in hard-edged metal, as geometric as can be. Where new materials and auxiliary architectural elements could not be seamlessly integrated, they are clearly and visibly distinguished, designed as a distinct and unusual form.

The final additions might indeed have succeeded in disturbing the self-contained impression, yet even these are integrated: wall lamps are mounted on rectangular metal plates, which in turn are set into the wall, as are the black horizontal rectangles of the light switches. Nothing is wantonly exposed; nothing is hidden, camouflaged, or masked. The technical installations do not disturb, but rather enrich the form, creating unity between old and new in their formal perfection. "I always try to integrate everything into the form, everything technically necessary", such as heating, lighting, closets. Technology disappears, but it is not camouflaged or hidden; rather, it is used in order to help attain the form.

(above) The former agricultural patio with its new additions: water acts as an element of rest, coolness and contemplation, while the elevator shaft's exaggerated proportions feel right for the space. (following page) The passage from the patio to the eastern terrace offers another place for cool breezes and reflections.

The large granite wall facing an open fireplace, behind which the kitchen lies, recalls Adolf Loos' maxim that the "meaning" of the modern decorative element should lie only in the material: "the work of art must be satisfied to bring out the material as much as possible." "What our time demands of ornament is a distilled preciousness, an extract of the noble." Outside as well, toward the esplanade, the kitchen is faced with a granite wall, or rather, a long, unadorned granite screen.

Much care was taken with the built-in wood furniture such as desks and cabinets, shelves and closets; they are perhaps most reminiscent of Louis Kahn. Both the built-in pieces and the free-standing furniture of oak and cherry wood were manufactured to specification. A trolley for the personnel was manufactured in series, as well as a screen. Those accustomed to thinking in simple oppositions will have a thing or two to learn here. The decisive vindication of early modernism is accompanied by Beaux-Arts typologies and images (which in fact were never entirely eradicated by modernism). Traditional typologies are evaluated for their suitability and interpreted. Undiluted modernism is applied in a way that does not exclude the consideration of individual scale and place. In Dos Santos' architecture, topographical or contextual limitations are welcomed and used as the point of departure for the design strategy, which is marked not by the schematic character of the International Style, but by the brilliant decisiveness of spirit of early modernism, with which great figures like Le Corbusier encouraged the younger generation of architects around the middle of the century. It should be remembered that in Portugal, the espousal of modernism had a specifically political and emancipatory significance for the architectural profession, constituting nothing less than the reclaiming of the architect's creative freedom. The position was less ideologically charged and less rigidly bound to social-political housing programs than in Germany, where modernism was more strongly equated with social-democratic moralism and formal freedom was instinctively associated with frivolity. In the meantime, however, the pathos has subsided even in Portugal, and the revisionist search for an allegedly authentic Portuguese architecture can be viewed more neutrally, fairly, and profitably from a distance. It is once again permissible to say in public that sometimes thick stone walls, small windows in massive masonry, solid socles and window frames are preferable to support-free glass, not only for reasons of durability and climate, but also because of the spatial feeling they evoke.

Less prominent monuments are more likely to permit an approach that combines the restoration of the old with a modern expansion. One should be especially thankful for such examples; rather than excusing the absence of new elements and counting on viewers to be overwhelmed with awe, they confront them with extensive interventions requiring much greater sensitivity on the part of the architect. For dos Santos, such projects are a welcome opportunity to demonstrate what he means when he says that he doesn't actually do anything. Such a claim represents neither false modesty nor mere understatement, but rather the arrogance of the perfectionist, the assurance of simply having avoided doing what was wrong, the security of having hit the right note. To quote Loos once more: "the aristocrats concerned themselves only with the material and the perfection of the work." Parvenues, on the other hand, want to distinguish themselves; they have so little individuality that they think they can show it off.

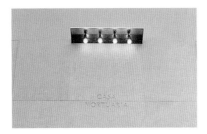

The renovation of the Pousada de Nossa Senhora da Assunção was preceded by a project comparable in many respects: the remodeling and expansion of the Palace Hotel do Bucaco. The entrance passage is dramatized by variations in ceiling height, descending stepwise in the small rooms and corridors. Toward the interior, the rooms become more and more compact, compressed, and subterranean, like a treasure vault. The vestibule and lavatories, dressing rooms, and cloakrooms show a Loosian compactness, reminiscent of Etruscan tombs, corresponding to the private character of these public facilities. They exude a preciousness like the dressing rooms of actresses, spaces of transformation, renewal, regeneration, recharging of batteries, the strength for leisure, the renewal of the enchantment, magical places where telluric energies are bundled. Here and in the guest baths, the viewer is overwhelmed by the marvelous patterns in the marble, conjured up by the cutting and reassembling of the stone according to the laws of repetition or opposition. The patterns show such bold coloration and are so large that they assert their own independence: they transgress the boundaries, constitute an autonomous field as in a painting by Klimt, usurp the motif, spread over different surfaces like a continuous sign, ignoring or evading the contours just as the unconscious evades the rational and space asserts itself against architecture. Here all the characteristics noted above in regard to the Pousada are already present. The elements tend to assume an independent form and detach themselves from the wall: the elevator and the television screen on the wall in the bar are like actors, mute servants, mannequins. Materials—palpable, perceptible—play a central role. Doors and windows are set into the wall with the precision of a safe. Alignments, lines of separation between marble and plaster, socle and floorboards, are continued or resumed; everything is connected and supplied by lines that reappear elsewhere, holding the room together in a strictly choreographed ballet.

The palace hotel, in turn, was preceded by the remodeling of a chapel into a mortuary. Unusually large areas of boldly-patterned Estremoz marble appear like Rorschach blots on folds of paper. The greenish lines, combined into X's and rhombuses, continue on the floor, while the interruption of the pattern in the corner only enhances the refinement. The chamfer makes it appear older, more aristocratic, more idiosyncratic, more spacious. The striped fabric of the chairs shows the same color range as the marble slabs—a stroke of Loosian boldness that at the same time recalls the Viennese workshops to which Loos was so vehemently opposed. The difference in the whole becomes negligible; the Viennese workshops return from their temporal distance to haunt Loos. The oversize patterning and the unprecedented chromatic audacity lend the walls and furniture a sense of indifference to their designated function, a certain autonomy, something rebellious. The agreement between the marble and the upholstery of the armchairs in the apse evokes the impression of an eerie arrangement, a secret metaphysical complicity behind human backs; God is in these stripes, in the labyrinth of patterns oblivious to contours and materials (and laughs at Loos).

The source of light cannot be exactly determined. It is Platonic light, the light of Suger's metaphysics, appearing to proceed from a glowing, illuminated wall. An outer limit deviating from the right angle makes space for the invisible source of light; the right angle itself is preserved by a half-lowered curtain that hides the source of illumination. The door in the corner (the side door from the autopsy room in the former chapel to the side rooms, as well as the freezer door) shows how this motif can function without the frame destroying the

effect, making it look like an accident, a debacle. It only works when the frame is omitted, when the jambs are flush with the wall, identical with it. Many features help imbue the space with its own existence; they show that the space is constituted not only by walls, floor, and ceiling, is not reducible to the sum of these coordinates, but has a life of its own, a previous existence endowed with its own meaning. The refinements bring the room to life. As with the direct power or magic of linguistic forms, there exists here a communication beyond semantics, emanating from the words themselves and the non-instrumental power of language. It is the aura exuded by singular names, isolated words from childhood experience, like the names in Karl May. The Surrealists invoked marginal linguistic phenomena, sacred or obscene—devotional forms, incantations, magic formulas, swear words, obscenities or insults, curses, spells; the Romantics wanted to use names like buttons. The focus is always the physiognomic content of the linguistic forms. One could speak of spatial forms in the same way: the physiognomy of magical linguistic energies, the Romantic discovery of a language of language, could correspond to the space of space. Karl Kraus said of language: "The closer one examines at a word, the further away it seems." In the same way, the more care is devoted to a design, the more precisely it is executed, the more enigmatic and puzzling the finished architecture seems. Absolute, obsessive precision is a technique for conjuring space. Novalis, thinking of a poetology of the autonomous reflexivity of linguistic forms, put it this way: "One can only admire that ridiculous error, when people imagine that they are speaking about the things. No one recognizes the very peculiarity of language, that it is concerned only with itself." Celan, too, spoke of the "fish-bones and membranes between the words." How could one assume that the architect's most important task is to provide space for necessary functions, to accommodate mundane courses of action and assign them a place, when it is perhaps rather to make visible and manifest the essence of the space, its secrets and beauty?

The exploration of these examples provides a background for evaluating dos Santos' most recent work, a daycare center in Berlin-Karow, only just completed. Surrounded by mediocre architecture in a new district with rowhouses and residential blocks—more like a village or a small town than the typical urban periphery—the daycare center stands out clearly, its planning investing it with a special status despite its low, almost stocky appearance, which is anything but ostentatious. The reserve and clarity of its formal language and the care taken in its design render it conspicuous already from a distance.

The staggered entrance front is oriented to the original building line of the neighboring residential structures, which, however, ended up being built further back than originally intended. The architect's efforts to embed the building volume in its context were thus thwarted by the context itself. The long east façade, faced in brick, is marked by two horizontal bands of windows, interrupted to the right and the left. The frames of the immovable windows are invisible from the exterior; only those of the square, adjustable windows can be seen. The vertical transoms in the horizontal window slits appear to stand behind the layer of brick; the glass pane behind forms a third layer.

The windows are framed below with zinc sheet metal and above with solid metal slabs (whose original thickness had to be reduced for reasons of cost), providing the unquiet brick opening with a precise edge. The effect of solid metal panel against stone was already

(previous page) Morgue, Lisbon: brass fixture for basic light bulbs at the entrance. (above) Brazões Wing, Palace Hotel, Buçaco: the intervention, banal in essence, consisted of removing excessive and purposeless interior elements in a building that had been left for years with no function.

(right) Kita-Karow, Berlin: detail of north façade, showing relation of the fixed frame to the movable frame with the mediation of disciplined brick courses. (following page) Plant room on the west façade, initially added as a mediating gesture of site alignments.

demonstrated by Souto de Moura in the courtyard of the cultural center of the Ministry of Culture in Porto——the hard contrast between the uneven stone and the metal, materials which, despite their incongruence, attempt almost painfully to conform to each other.

The east side and the angled south side, self-contained with strictly arranged windows, extend around the building like a protective rear guard, while the classrooms open toward the courtyard. The unprotected west side appears as if unfolded and opened outward (like a parasol bent saucily upwards); the roof overhang is as wide as the continuous balcony. Windows and wood surfaces lie in a single plane, while the doors are slightly recessed. Wood and glass form near squares; the profiles are as narrow as possible.

Closed, with lowered visor, the mute imprint of interior life, or unabashedly open, incorporating the surroundings: these are modernism's two answers to the problem of the façade. Surfaces are decisive for the solidity of the outer skin, clearly contoured, uninterrupted surfaces. Dos Santos' facades sometimes show the superhuman, involuntary, unconsciously machine-like precision of early modernism, though tempered by the warm brick, and in Arraiolos muted by the Mediterranean idiom. The actual façade parlante of the daycare center is the roof: from the air, it looks like an El Lissitzky.

Two building sections, very different in character, are clearly distinguished from one another: brick for the administration, wood and glass for the classrooms. There the power of brick ends. The connection is light and transparent, a sluice through which the gaze can pass unhindered to the sides. The whole sometimes shows Loos' "certain pleasure in compactness" (Moneo), sometimes it is as expansive as Wright's prairie houses, thanks to an open design method like that of Aalto, marked by the articulation and displacement of structures.

The actual façade is the east side, not the side where the entrance is. On the entrance side, moreover, the entrance is not in the middle, but is shifted out of the central axis in a game of displacements. That much is Loos: the distinction between right and left, continuing on the interior. Nor does the movement from front to back run along the central axis, but is rerouted to one of the two sides. This building shows a bias toward the right which, in combination with the stair-climbing, generates a spiral movement. On the interior, the entrance is framed by a cube that seems like a piece of furniture set into the space. The walls are painted sky blue, thus reinforcing the impression that they continue beyond the cube, a feeling irreconcilable with the knowledge that the door leads to the outside. In the service hallway, the room height changes. The static perspective of the wide angle camera does not adequately convey the sequential character of the spaces as experienced by the visitor passing through them, with surprises around every corner. The building is oriented not to the optically centered architecture of the Baroque, but more to the Arabic, from which, as Le Corbusier said, we can learn a great deal, since it favors the act of walking, of movement from one place to another in the experience of the articulation of architecture.

Muthesius, whose writings repeatedly invoke the model of the English country house, had a fair amount to say on the aesthetic value of varying room heights, an idea Loos carried to its conclusion in the concept of the Raumplan——the height of the room as an important

element in its unique effect. Here, however, the notion of a Raumplan is approached with irony as well: a bathroom doesn't need to be as high as a hall, but in the day care center it is just that high—not only to provide daylight, but also because of the surprising chimney-like effect. The too-high bathroom as a negative result of the correctly proportioned hall, however, is viewed not as a deficiency, but as an opportunity.

Door frames and window profiles are always flush with the wall. Doors are repeatedly tucked into corners, sucked in by them, as it were, resulting in a strangely puzzling geometry. In a lecture, Souta de Moura once said that architectural history is the history of baseboards. Like door frames, they exist to cover imperfection, for example of the line between the wall and the floor. Doors have always been placed in the center of walls, never in the corner, so that frames could be placed around them. Perfection requires a challenge; corner doors require perfection.

The division of the architectural volume into two structures placed across the corner got some tension through the displacement of the access corridors away from the cross axes. Despite clear articulation, axiality and symmetries are difficult to discern. The space is more than enterability and permeability. At the beginning of the hallway, a staircase with a landing leads to the upper story. The wall between the two flights of stairs stands free, like a piece of furniture in the space, lending the stairway self-sufficiency as a free-standing element. The space is drawn into it in a spiral movement. Here the stereometries of differing widths, heights, and shades of white suggest a Cubist image. Such painterly effects are not the primary intention, "but I like accidents. A building without drama is nothing." Happy accidents like these, however, require clean and precise craftsmanship, an aspect with which the architect was not always content in this building.

(above) Kita-Karow: entrance niche of the children's bathrooms. It is easier to obtain rigor in the assembly of a Volkswagen than in the laying of tiles today, given the state of the German building industry. (following page, left) Entrance vestibule looking toward supervisor's office, dividing wall and exterior gap between the entrance and classroom buildings (following page, right) Interior of classroom with built-in toy storage disguised behind a mirrored screen.

In the upper story, the hall is illuminated by skylights whose domes are larger than the openings and whose sides are so high that unless one stands directly beneath them, it is impossible to see where the light is coming from. The slits of light rhythmically punctuate the hallway like apparitions. The element "fixed window/niche/movable window" in the teachers' lounges—first used in the house in Luso and developed further in the convent (where it was interpreted in accord with the traditional niches of the monks, accommodating a desk)—here serves as a storage niche.

In a certain sense, there are no details: everything is integrated into the overall form. Even technical installations that stubbornly resist the architecture are developed until they no longer hinder the form, but enrich it. The aesthetic implications of the standard range of technical and comfort facilities are largely neutralized.

Dissatisfaction with standard products, however, does not necessarily mean the propagation of special designs, as in the artistically ennobled handwork of Jugendstil. On the contrary, as with Le Corbusier and Adolf Loos, the goal is the banal, void of artistic intention, for architecture proceeds from the rules of good craftsmanship. In Portugal, manufacture to specification and special production are

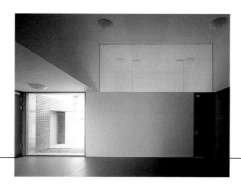 

considerably more affordable than in Germany, and craftspeople are more open to deviation from the standard line of products. They are not yet so far removed from their tradition; they are more likely to integrate the industrial serial product into their tradition than to feel relieved of the necessity to put mental effort into its creation. In Dos Santos' opinion, there is such a thing as good craftsmanship and basic rules for architecture; not every generation or every building project has to reinvent the wheel. At first, dos Santos was persuaded of the superiority of a developed industrial nation and sure of finding better conditions there. Since then, he has come to see things in a different light: now to him technological backwardness seems to represent a favorable precondition for good architecture. Loos once said that if craftsmen were only permitted to work in the style of their time, they would be always modern and need no architects. Nowadays, we need architects to teach the craftspeople their craft.

What is at stake is the development of practical solutions—not in the sense of beautification or decoration, or of conscious artistic design, but of a satisfactory design solution to the formal problems posed, for example, by modern domestic engineering. This constitutes proof of the connection between architecture and design—no longer an omnipotent design fantasy extending from the form of the city to that of the door handle in the sense of a gesamtkunstwerk, but an idea of culture embracing everything done by inhabitants, owners, and craftsmen on a day-to-day basis. The construction industry, do-it-yourself industry, and furniture industry play a crucial role in this process, definitively setting the aesthetic standards, i.e., keeping them at a low level. Most architects are not interested in this process, and it is rarely expected of them. Loos wanted to exclude the artist from the design of such functional objects on principle. Muthesius, on the other hand, in a position that seems more tenable to me, adopted the hypothesis of an instinctive design or "naïve artistic vision," urging the applied artist to once again seize upon these natural abilities and design principles for the "construction of an artistic culture." Like Loos, one may conceive of form as the collective work of humanity, making individual attempts to invent it meaningless. Yet where this process shows gaps or differences in level, the architect as an individual may be able to suggest a more refined solution. This attunement, this integration, this perfection does not imply the domination of the inhabitant by the architect in a space whose perfection makes dwelling as stressful as it would be to sit for a month in Tristan and Isolde. Rather, it serves to make disruptive elements bearable; dos Santos' goal is to arrange and design the elements in such a way that they get along well with each other.

As far as sources of inspiration are concerned, Adolf Loos again and again comes immediately to mind. In fact, Loos is such an obvious choice that he is actually a red herring, like an obvious suspect in a bad detective novel. Loos' houses are oriented to the English country house with its development from the small cottage to the manor, and so for dos Santos, his Raumplan resembles a series of additions, the house for three generations (Loos is the father who keeps adding to his house so that children and grandchildren will stay at home). Dos Santos' model is less the bourgeois country house or the architectural studio, than the aristocratic palace.

The Paris hôtel particulier, made an early impression on him and contributed essentially to the development of a pronounced sense of spatial order, making it conscious and comprehensible to him. "I have a strange sense of order." Dos Santos likes to see spaces arranged

hierarchically. The hôtel particulier is characterized by the artful variation of fixed rules. "It is like a game—hierarchies and symmetries are everywhere, but they are not apparent; the game remains a secret one". The typological vocabulary of the Beaux-Arts school has long been denigrated, all too vehemently and simplistically. Axes and symmetries were reified and denounced as the destruction of freedom and the symptom of paralysis. Yet freedom can still be enjoyed within the boundaries of the metier, within the framework of the rules. Indeed, the constraints of the rules heighten the pleasure of the violation. Enjoyment presupposes the validity of strict rules.

Dos Santos sees the traditional in the modern and the modern prefigured in the traditional. What interests him is the communication between the two, e.g. Mies' early Haus Riehl or Behrens' Haus Wiegand as response to the type of the Schinkel villa preserved a sense of order and hierarchy. The process of breaking open the self-contained ground plan expands the possibilities. The same kind of circulation—leading from room to room, arising from the interpenetration of individual spaces—and the organic arrangement of space that had earlier prevailed in office buildings is found in the old monasteries as well.

In the search for models, one should look to Louis Kahn. One should observe the way in which he divides up areas, frames them, contrasts materials, sets windows and doors flush into the wall, cuts angles, juxtaposes wood areas with ceiling-high windows and combines built-in cabinets with windows and doors, the way reading niches are incorporated into the wall, or observe his monumental lighting.

Dos Santos says that he enters competitions more for the sake of training and experience than from the hope of gaining a commission; and so he participates even when the chance of winning is negligible. His constant concern is to develop a clear concept for the problem posed. His competition entries are concepts, only diagrams, but elaborated enough to see that most of dos Santos' building types— school, campus, boarding school, parliament, daycare center, hotel, morgue—constitute a strange unity. All are places where social life is subjected to special rules, to a certain degree of de-individualization; perhaps for this very reason, nearly all are places of an Arcadian lifestyle and can be traced back to the model of the Phalanstère. Their architectural delimitation postulates a certain seclusion as a quality of existence, a "pleasure in being" (R. Barthes). Even the entering and traversing of the building are presented as a journey, an initiation; the architecture marks the beginning and end of a journey. Every harmonization of parts feared to be irreconcilable, each disclosure of the seemingly heterogeneous as similar is experienced as a pleasant relief. The task of the applied artist is to economize, harmonize, and organize thoughts and forms, to provide a comfortable resting place for the mind—the non-contradiction of dress coat and façade with Loos, of elevator or light switch and interior with dos Santos. The way in which things don't call attention to themselves is in itself worthy of attention—as if the camera lens were focused with particular sharpness. Dos Santos' architecture is soothing and cheering because it conveys the impression that all problems can be solved, that no compromises are necessary, that the idea was preserved and emerged victorious. It suggests that the architect can do anything—the contingent is robbed of its power, just like that.

(previous page, left) Tourist Office, Luso: "endless" counter is simultaneously a niche, an inglenook, a bookshelf, and an information desk, ending only on a mezzanine level where it houses books for the local children. (previous page, right) Stone slabs resting on vertical stacks in a cemetery lost in the countryside. (left) House in Pego: "Accidental" façade at bedrooms, to be further developed in subsequent works. (following spread, left) Kita-Karow: balcony.

Works ▶

House in Pego

In Pego, a small rural village, a house "banal" in essence is the outcome of a project done on precarious and unexpected terms. The house was built from a very rough sketch proposal and without a proper design—not to mention drawings—to support it. Once the skeleton was built, details were drawn on a daily basis at the insistence of the owner (who, incidentally, was the insurance broker for the office).

The program was for a three-bedroom house, on quite a steep and narrow site. The extremely tight budget required frugal detailing. Windows were made according to the size of the couple; doors to the height of beams and slabs. The volume has the generosity of the section.

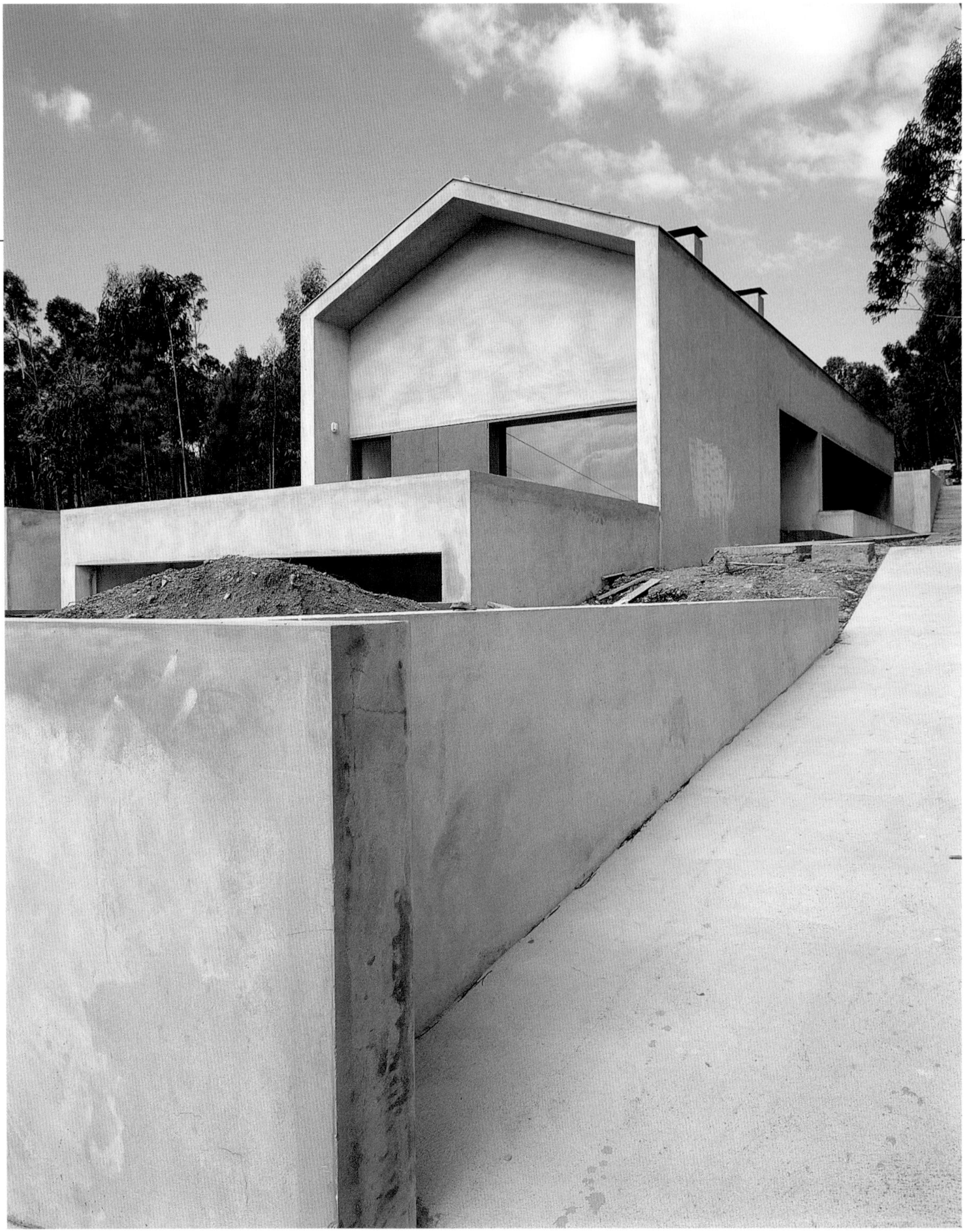

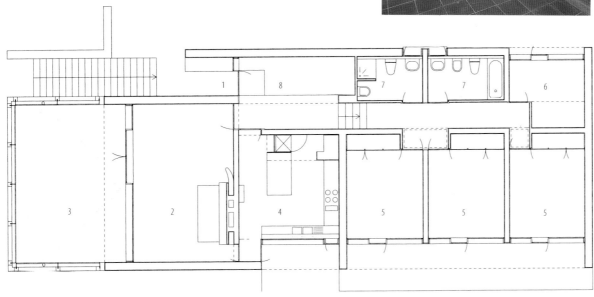

FLOOR PLAN

1 ENTRANCE
2 LIVING ROOM
3 TERRACE
4 KITCHEN
5 BEDROOM
6 STUDIO OFFICE
7 BATHROOM
8 VESTIBULE

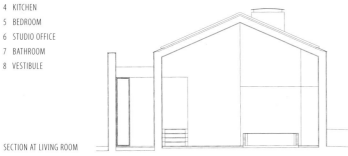

SECTION AT LIVING ROOM

(previous spread) The house in Pego, totally "accidental" from its inception, sits on a sloping and very narrow, long plot of land in pine woods. First thought to be a chapel by the inhabitants of the area, no one would believe that its simple forms, reminiscent of local vernacular architecture, could accommodate spaces of varying proportions. While the house sits gently on the slope, an industrious machine operator decided to open his way through the site with his machine, its "footprint" becoming the garage access. (this spread) South and east façades showing the symmetric-asymmetric main window layout.

(this page, top and bottom, following page) The east façade, with opening for the bedrooms to the right and for the kitchen to the left. (this page, middle) Interior of bedrooms, looking out.

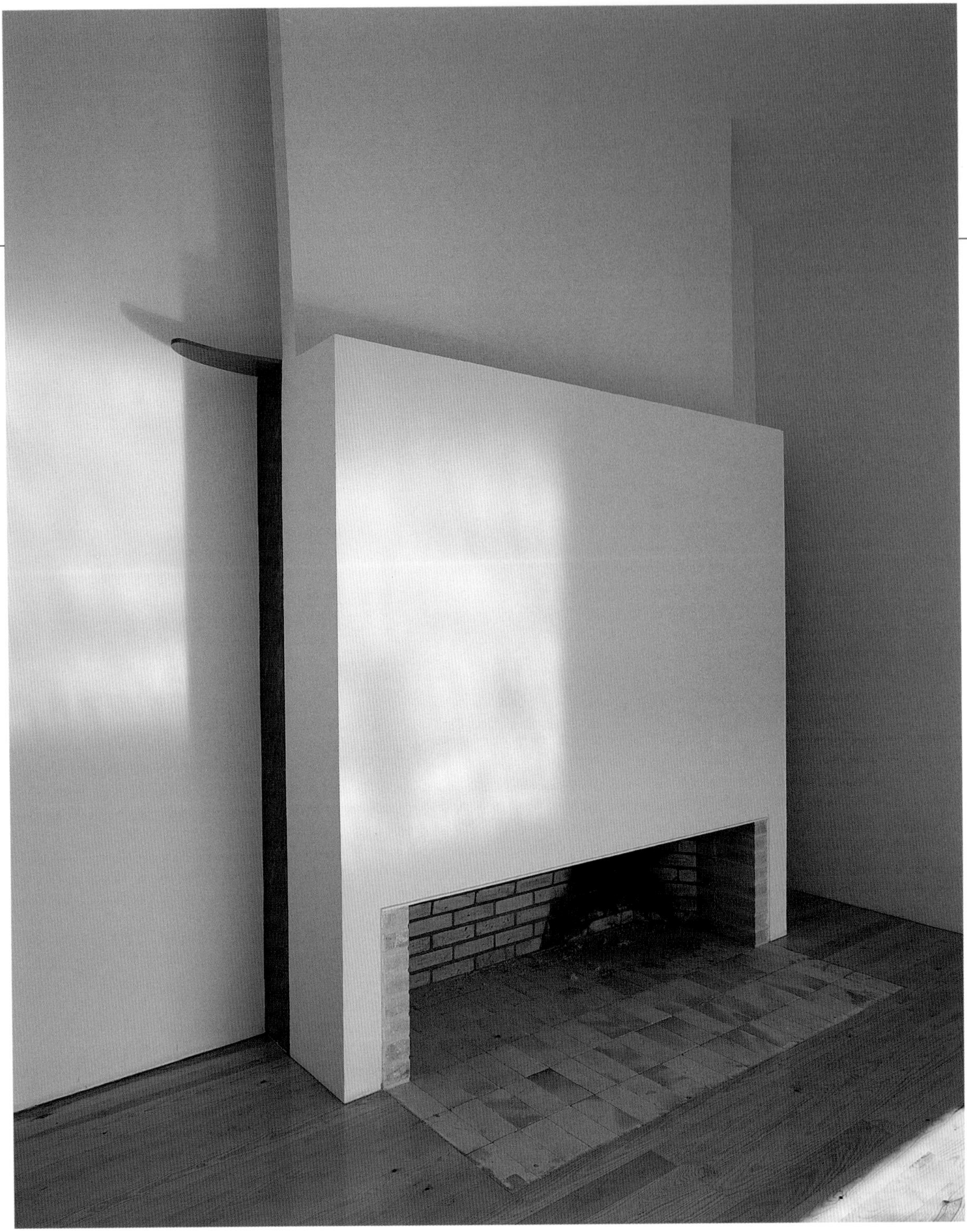

(previous spread) Detail at main opening in the living area, looking toward the terrace. A game of proportions and alignments was implemented while the wood in stock held out—the available cedar was just enough for the previous bedroom area and this one. (this spread) Views of the living area where an enormous casing houses not only the fireplace for this room but another one behind, in the kitchen, used for cooking. Their alignments and misalignments are only barely discernible.

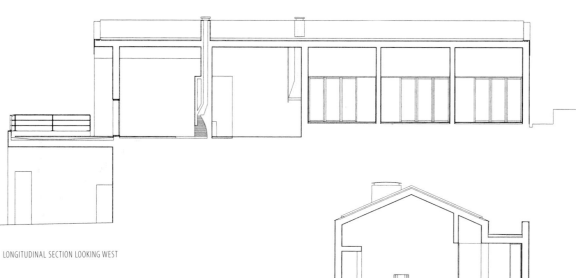

LONGITUDINAL SECTION LOOKING WEST

(right and far right) The kitchen fireplace, behind and higher than the fireplace in the living area, features cantilevered bricks in precarious balance. (above) The main door and frame into the vestibule were created with scarce means from another available lot of wood.

TRANSVERSE SECTION THROUGH KITCHEN WITH FIREPLACE ELEVATION

TRANSVERSE SECTION THROUGH KITCHEN AND CORRIDOR TO BEDROOMS

(far left) View of bedroom looking
to door and closets, with pine on the
floor and mahogany veneer on the
door panels. (left) Sequential views
of the access to the bedrooms from
the vestibule. The budget size disallow
a false ceiling to conceal unwanted
structural beams.

Tourist Office Refurbishment

In the small spa town of Luso, a tourist information center was to be accommodated. The building allocated for this purpose, a vacant primary school, was to house additional facilities for public use as well: a small library, a room for exhibitions, and restrooms. The building was left basically intact. Interior circulation was a primary issue: the public circulate on, as it were, the outer edge of the building, while staff move nearer its core.

The only visible element that was added, a wall hiding a gallery, structures the newly formed space, which is punctuated by a series of spatial "accidents". Another element—freestanding—containing shelving for the small library and odd objects, organizes a room for exhibitions and related events.

Adjacent to the existing building, a new structure will house a projection room accessible both from the tourist office and directly from the exterior.

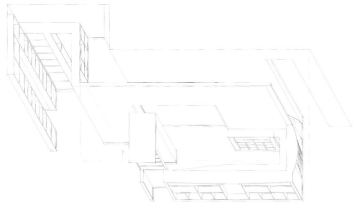

NEW GROUND FLOOR PLAN WITH PROPOSED PROJECTION
PAVILION FLOOR PLAN AND AXONOMETRIC (CENTER AND RIGHT)

1 ENTRY   5 EXHIBITION HALL
2 VESTIBULE   6 PROJECTION ROOM
3 TOURIST OFFICE   7 STAFF AREA
4 READING ROOM   8 GALLERY (MEZZANINE)

SIDE ELEVATION WITH PROJECTION PAVILION (ABOVE)

MAIN AND SIDE ELEVATION (LEFT AND ABOVE)

EXISTING GROUND FLOOR PLAN

NEW MEZZANINE LEVEL

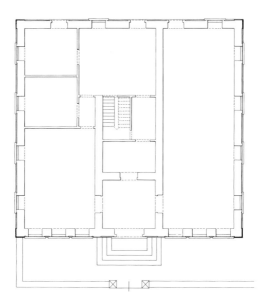

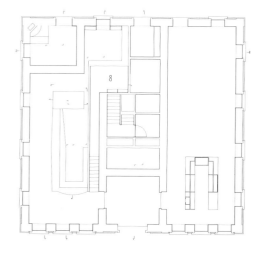

(previous spread and this spread) This initial work gave the opportunity to consider the material quality inherent in a place, including careful evaluation of possible existing relationships—axes, alignments, the fusing of old and new. A composite element was created to organize and structure the space all on its own, having its own hierarchical rules, being simple but also warm, rigorous but with enough tolerance to feel right to the emotions without feeling wrong to a sense of reality. (left) Tourist counter and access to mezzanine level (left above) overlooking the main room.

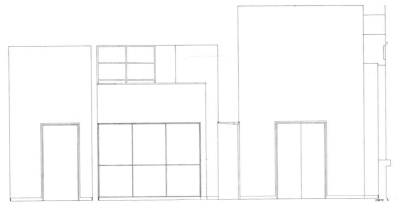

SECTION AT READING ROOM

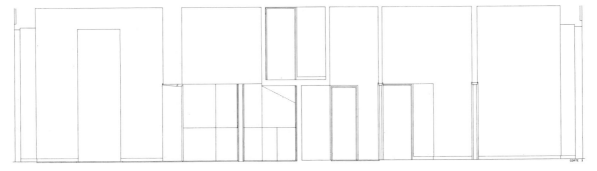

SECTION AT READING ROOM

(far left) Volumetric relationships on a continuum capable of offering different states of spatial perception are intriguing and fascinating, from the early development of the English country house to its modern, more rational successors like the haus Moller or the haus Muller. On the mezzanine a low-ceilinged (1.80 meters; 6 feet) platform in the children's reading area accommodates under it, next to the book storage, an inglenook of reduced volumetric proportions, part of the adult reading area. (left) Detail of the niche as part of the freestanding, organizing element, never touching the existing walls.

(right) View of the tourist office counter from its interior. On the right, the underside of the mezzanine level and the visible mahogany that was utilized throughout the entire work except for the pine floor. (far right) The tourist office counter from the exterior, with the telephone booth and seat with cover mediating the staff access to the public zones.

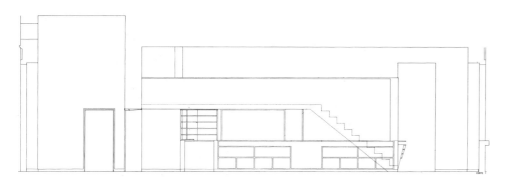

SECTION THROUGH TOURIST OFFICE

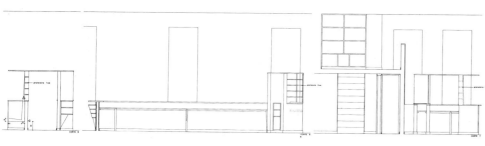

SECTION THROUGH TOURIST OFFICE

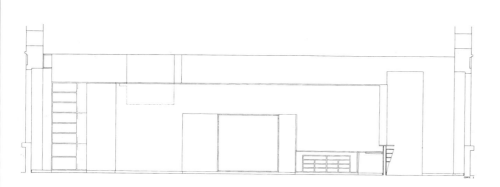

SECTION THROUGH READING ROOM

(far right) The entrance hall, with stone cladding and flooring. (right, top) Existing fireplace and sink (at sill, to left) uncovered during demolition. (right, middle) An early sketch proposal that did not take into account the corner fireplace. (right, bottom) Entrance to public restroom.

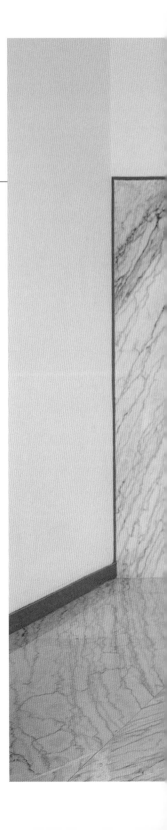

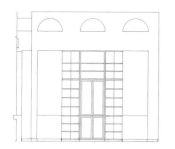

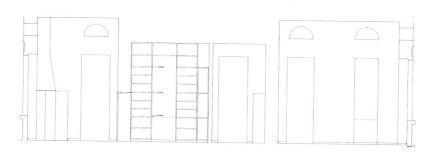

ELEVATION AND SECTION THROUGH EXHIBITION HALL

(left and far left) A shelving unit that is a piece of furniture intended to reorder and give sequence to a room used for more than one function, acting to divide the entrance hall from the main exhibition and secondary reading areas.

Autopsy Room and Morgue

LISBON, PORTUGAL

The intention of the project was the renovation and extension of the pathology department of the Curry Cabral Hospital in Lisbon. The existing building comprised three wings in poor condition. Two were used for laboratories; the other was used for the conservation and preparation of cadavers, autopsy rooms, and a chapel.

The project places laboratories and related paraphernalia (i.e., spaces for electronic microscopy, scientific photography, cytology, immunocitochemistry, and so on) in the first two wings. A zone for the conservation and preparation of cadavers, the autopsy room (in the former chapel), a laboratory for the registration of body parts, changing rooms for the staff, and a pathology museum are all located in the third wing. The zone for the conservation and preparation of cadavers had to be physically separated from the autopsy room; this was achieved by building a "tunnel-fridge," where bodies wait to be operated on, between the two areas.

In addition to the renovated areas, a new hospital morgue was constructed adjacent to the existing building, with a room for dressing corpses, a zone for coffins (with special lighting), a place for families to attend ceremonies, and support facilities. A garden for the morgue is strictly separated from the hospital, although access is possible. The new building has a false wall next to it to provide shade in the room for the conservation of cadavers.

In order to respect the limited budget, common building materials were employed except in special zones—the autopsy room and the morgue—where inexpensive Estremoz marble was used.

EXISTING CONDITIONS

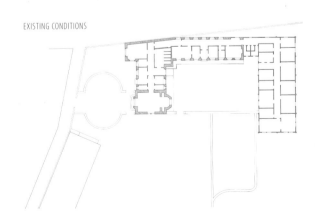

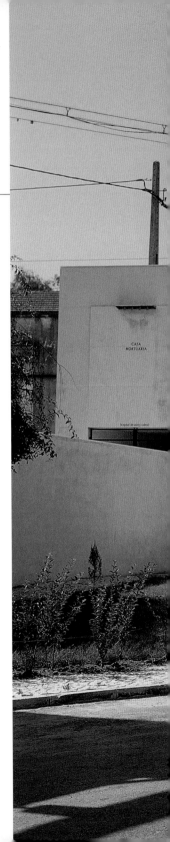

CASA
MORTUÁRIA

hospital de curry cabral

(previous spread) The façade of the new
morgue in relation to the former chapel,
now an autopsy room. (right) Main
entrance to the morgue, now completely
separated from the hospital campus.

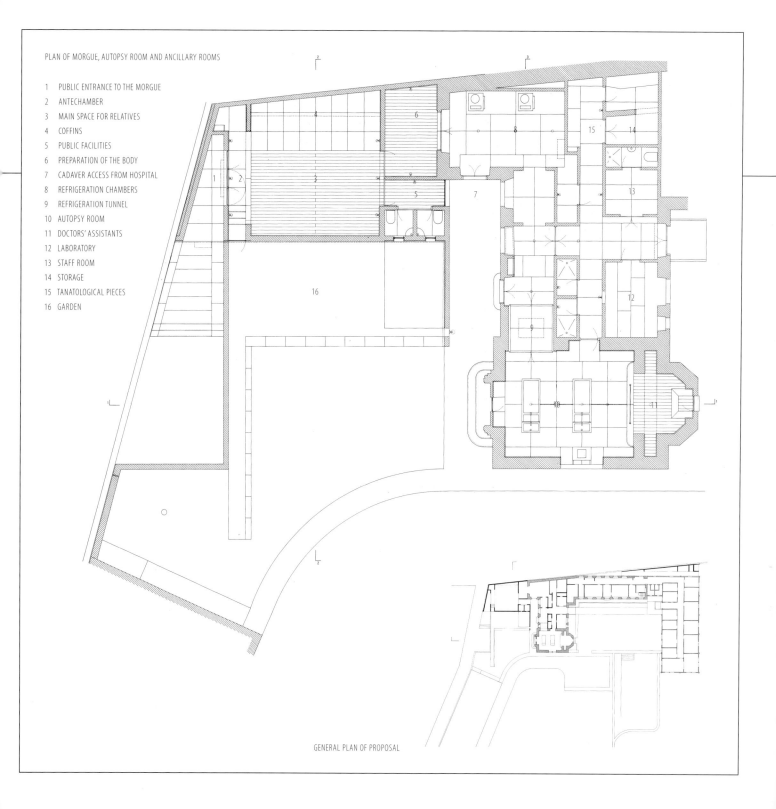

PLAN OF MORGUE, AUTOPSY ROOM AND ANCILLARY ROOMS

1 PUBLIC ENTRANCE TO THE MORGUE
2 ANTECHAMBER
3 MAIN SPACE FOR RELATIVES
4 COFFINS
5 PUBLIC FACILITIES
6 PREPARATION OF THE BODY
7 CADAVER ACCESS FROM HOSPITAL
8 REFRIGERATION CHAMBERS
9 REFRIGERATION TUNNEL
10 AUTOPSY ROOM
11 DOCTORS' ASSISTANTS
12 LABORATORY
13 STAFF ROOM
14 STORAGE
15 TANATOLOGICAL PIECES
16 GARDEN

GENERAL PLAN OF PROPOSAL

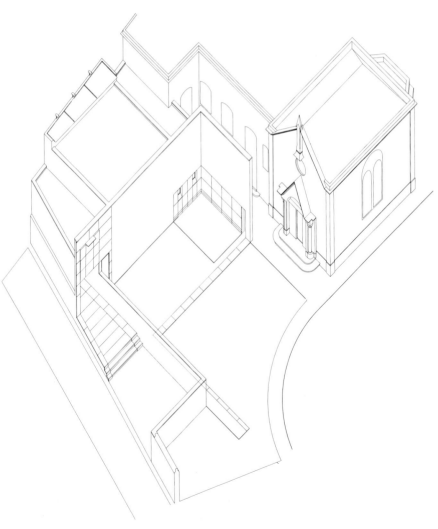

(above and right) The formality of the garden is intended to accommodate new kinds of rituals, to create a place for relatives to wander in sorrow, but in nature, as opposed to previous areas for the rituals of condolence. (far right) Previous axis to the chapel/autopsy room is deliberately interrupted by the new garden.

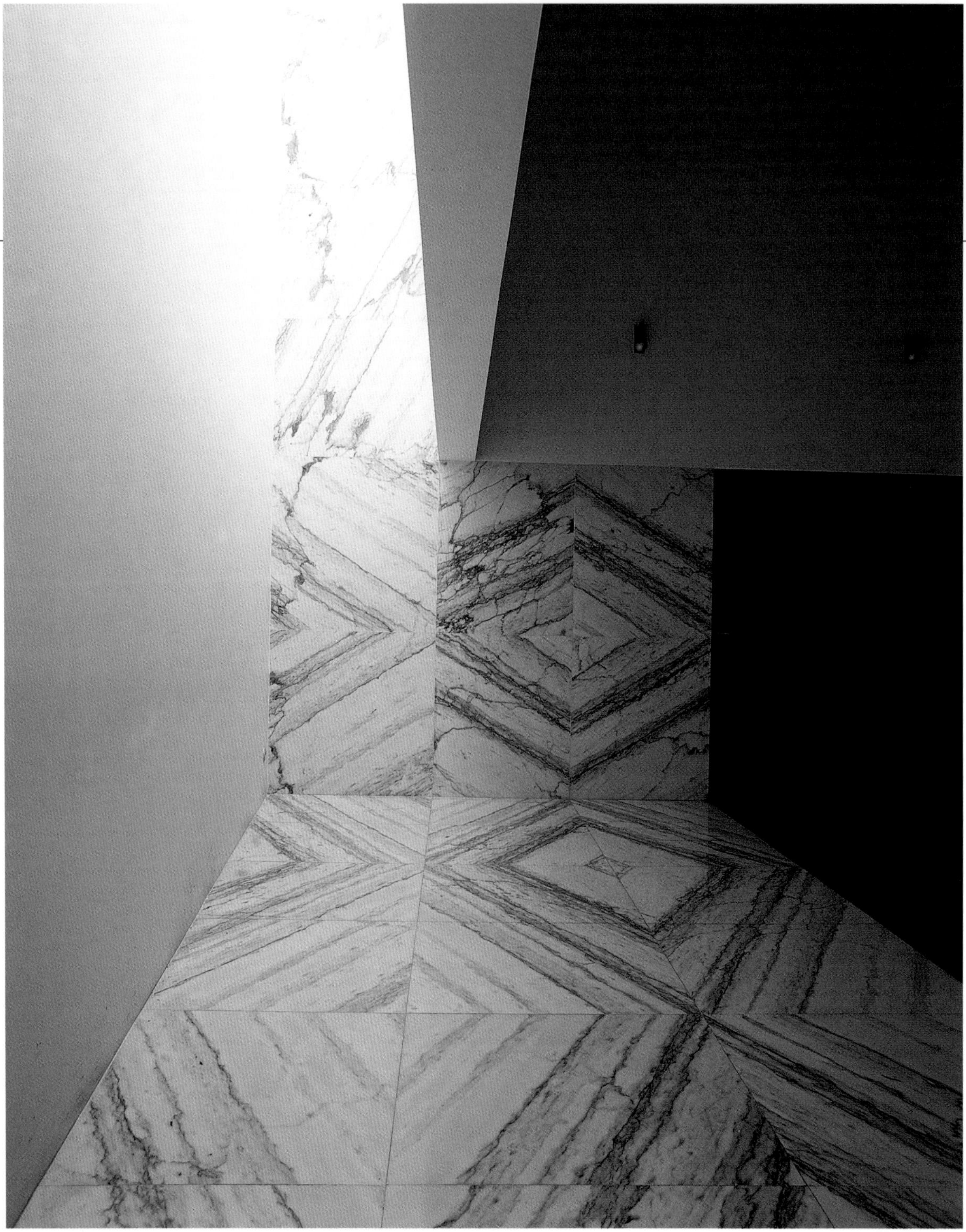

SECTION THROUGH MORGUE

(previous spread and this spread)
Morgue interior. Not only the material
quality of a room but also its system
of volumetric relationships are capable
of moving the senses—or, in the
case of this room, imposing an attitude
of reflection. Light and shadow, lowness
and ethereal height coexist in this
tight room.

Autopsy Room and Morgue

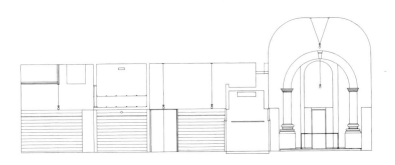

SECTION THROUGH AUTOPSY ROOM (FORMERLY THE CHAPEL)

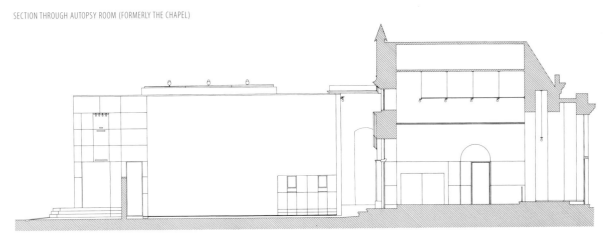

SECTION THROUGH AUTOPSY ROOM WITH MORGUE ELEVATION

(left) The new autopsy room subverts
the former character of the chapel and
its rituals. Instead of the confessional,
a refrigerated tunnel keeps corpses
ready for the autopsy operations that
take place in the main area, with the
"pulpit" now occupied by the assisting
physician, who comes to confirm his—
probably wrong—diagnosis.

Palace Hotel Buçaco Renovation

BUÇACO, PORTUGAL

The Palace Hotel do Buçaco, which was not originally built as a hotel, is composed of various wings—Palácio, Pedrinhas, Brazões, Cedros—displaying a wild mixture of architectural styles. The project called for the renovation and restructuring of the entire Brazões wing and basement, the ground floor and partial first floor of the Pedrinhas wing, and a covered passage between the Palácio and Brazões wings. Due to their poor condition, these portions of the hotel had been totally abandoned.

The Brazões building consists of three floors, to which a mezzanine level was added for service. On the lowest level of this building a series of rooms was created for public functions: meeting rooms, a bar, and restrooms. The upper two levels were used for hotel guest rooms, not uniformly shaped, due to existing conditions. An existing stair—where structural stone was revealed to give a window a different reading—and a new elevator link all floors.

In this delicate—if rather kitsch—structure, an effort was made to single out existing elements of construction that would lend coherence to the building, with the new intervention based on discretely plain elements. (Prior to the project, a multitude of disconnected finishes were to be found in some rooms.) Special care was taken with the new public areas on the ground floor: marble, oak and unpolished local limestone—with careful study of stone cutting—were used, as well as subtle differentiation in the colors of the stucco. The guest room baths, though small in scale, are quite playful. While a single rule for the layout of the marble slabs is maintained, there is a degree of variation in the volume of the bathrooms through changing ceiling heights. In the Pedrinhas wing, a service area at a lower level allows room on the ground floor for more guest rooms, as well as a public room without a specific purpose. This part of the hotel is also served by an existing stair and a new elevator.

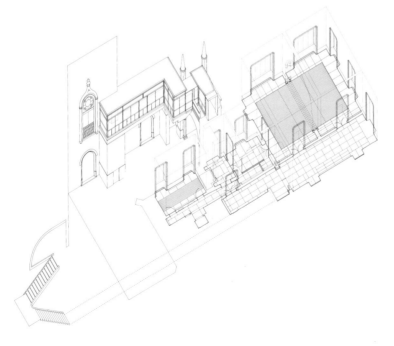

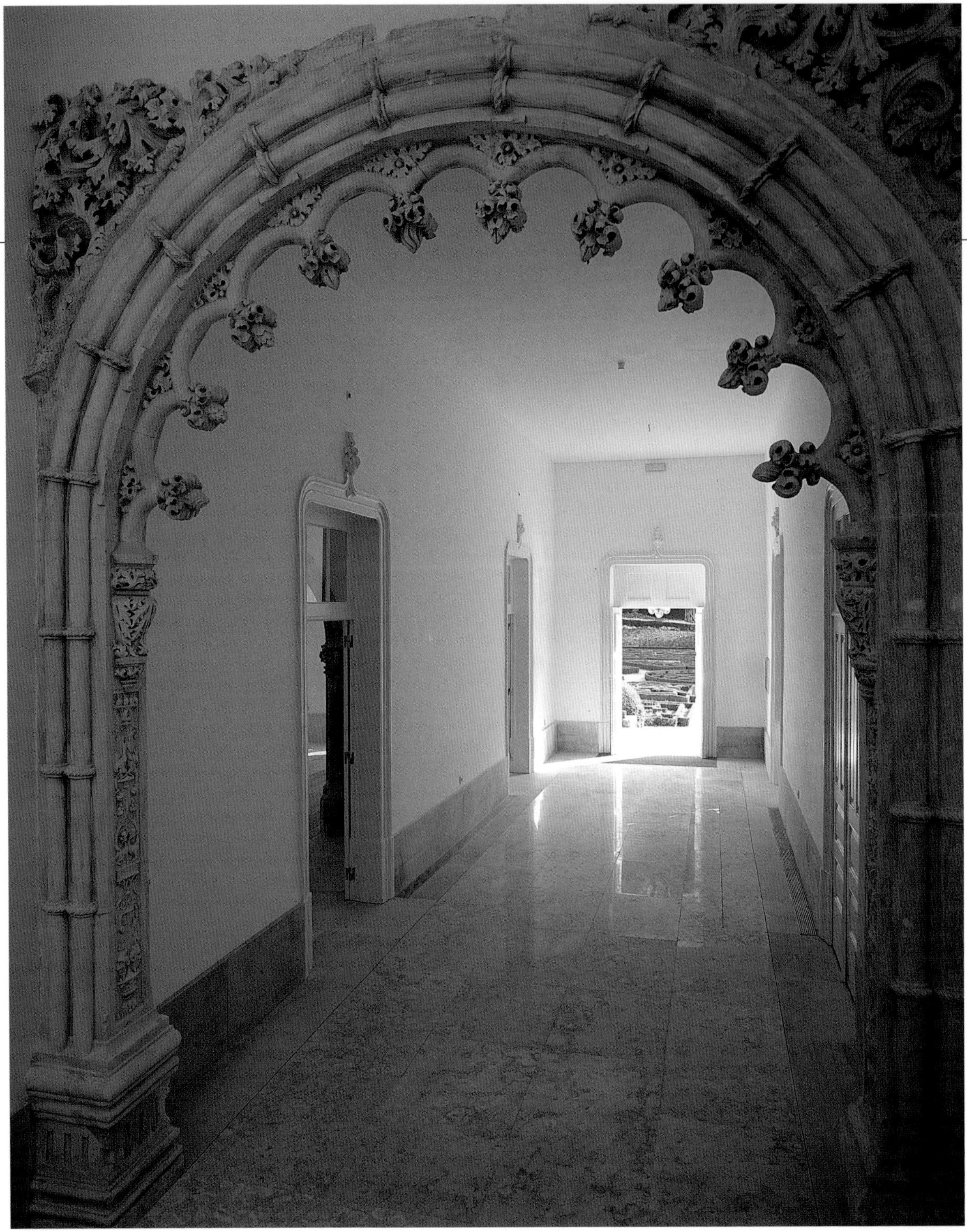

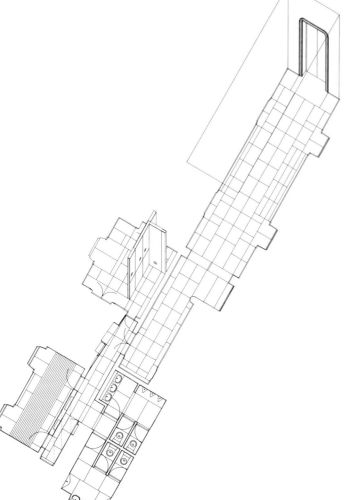

(previous spread, right) The Palace Hotel from the south. The Brazões wing is in the foreground; the Palacio is to the right; to the left, further in the background, is the roof of the Pedrinhas wing, barely visible. (previous spread, left) Entrance to the meeting room in the Pedrinhas wing, the only visible sign of intervention from the exterior, with a simple set of openings set to fit within the existing arch, formerly used as storage area. (this spread) Access corridors and stair of the Brazões wing, where an effort was made to soften elaborate recent stucco work so that the original stone work could be seen on its own.

Palace Hotel Buçaco Renovation

GROUND FLOOR PLAN

FIRST FLOOR PLAN

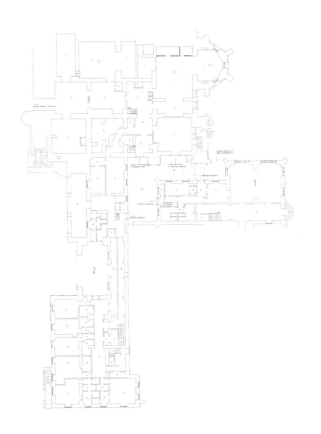

1 BRAZOES WING
2 PEDRINHAS WING
3 PALACIO
4 MAIN HOTEL ENTRANCE
5 ENTRANCE TO BRAZOES

(far left, above) Multipurpose room.
(left) Beyond the multipurpose room access to the elevator is through an anteroom that hides a coat rack and small service bar behind a stone screen. In addition to efforts to reduce the heaviness of the existing ornamentation, care was also taken to locate discreetly all the technical paraphernalia necessary for modern hotel functions.

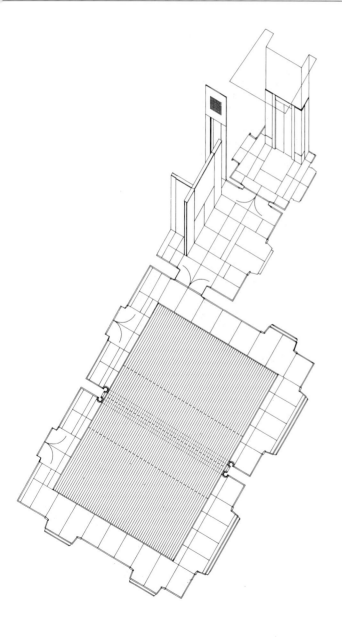

(far left and axonometric) View of the ancillary room connected to the conference room and the ground level elevator lobby beyond. The ancillary room serves as a bar-passage with the elevator at the far end. It was built with coarsely sawn slabs of local sandstone. (top and middle left) Elevator at main hotel level with both solid and thin slabs of sandstone used as revetment for the outside of the shaft. (bottom left) Elevator at ground level with the bar-passage in the foreground.

Palace Hotel Buçaco Renovation

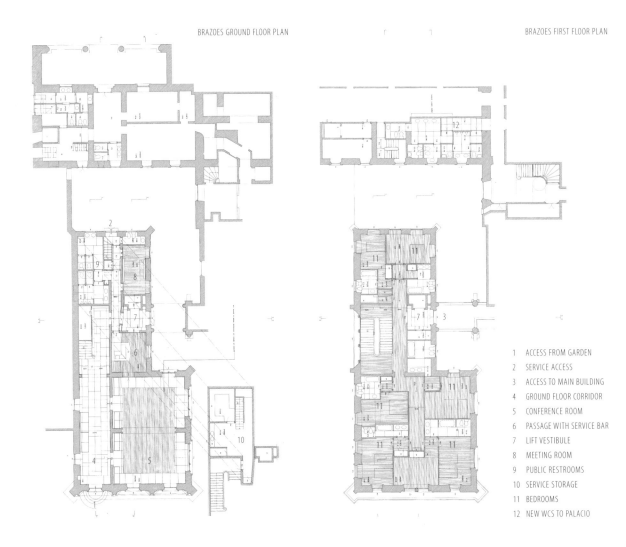

BRAZOES GROUND FLOOR PLAN

BRAZOES FIRST FLOOR PLAN

1   ACCESS FROM GARDEN
2   SERVICE ACCESS
3   ACCESS TO MAIN BUILDING
4   GROUND FLOOR CORRIDOR
5   CONFERENCE ROOM
6   PASSAGE WITH SERVICE BAR
7   LIFT VESTIBULE
8   MEETING ROOM
9   PUBLIC RESTROOMS
10 SERVICE STORAGE
11 BEDROOMS
12 NEW WCS TO PALACIO

(left and opposite, above) The only evident intervention is a freestanding stone screen in an anteroom that serves as a corridor and service preparation area. The stone is judiciously used and detailed as revetment, not structure.

(right) Pedrinhas wing, where a labyrinthine corridor occupying former interior spaces leads to a series of guest bedrooms and to the public meeting room at the end. (far right, left) Meeting room, with simple slabs of sandstone and pine on the floor and a false ceiling hiding existing unremovable service equipment for the upper part of the building. (far right, middle) The corridor towards the guest rooms. (far right, right) The end of the corridor with access to a public stair.

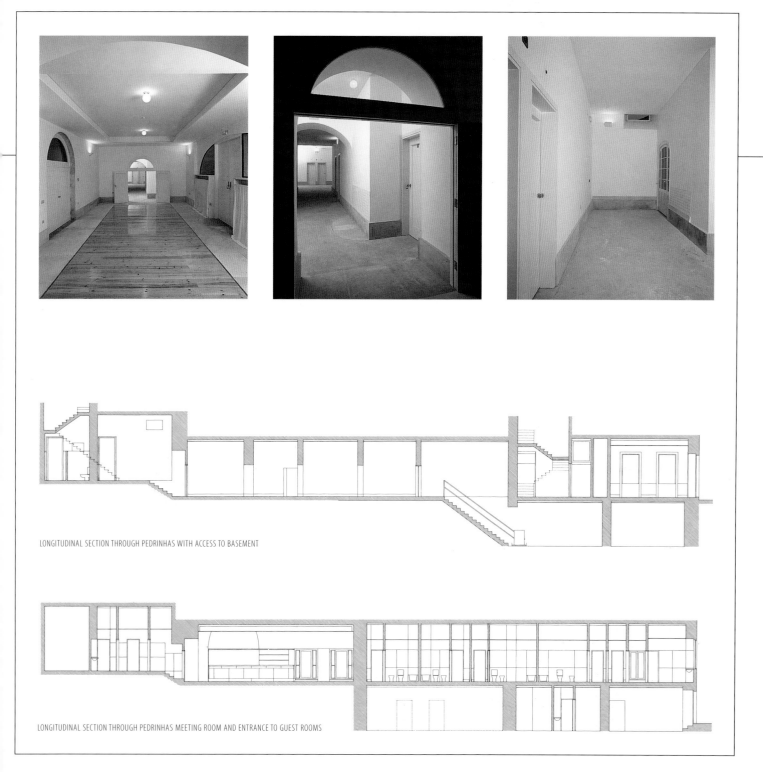

LONGITUDINAL SECTION THROUGH PEDRINHAS WITH ACCESS TO BASEMENT

LONGITUDINAL SECTION THROUGH PEDRINHAS MEETING ROOM AND ENTRANCE TO GUEST ROOMS

(right, top) Detail, guest bathroom. (right, middle and bottom) Entrance and detail at ground-level public restroom in the Brazões wing. (far right) Bathrooms for the hotel guest rooms in the Brazões wing form a playful sequence of spaces volumetrically broken into various parts, with the upper line of the marble wainscoting unifying the whole.

SECTIONS TROUGH BRAZOES

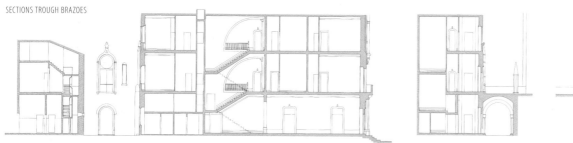

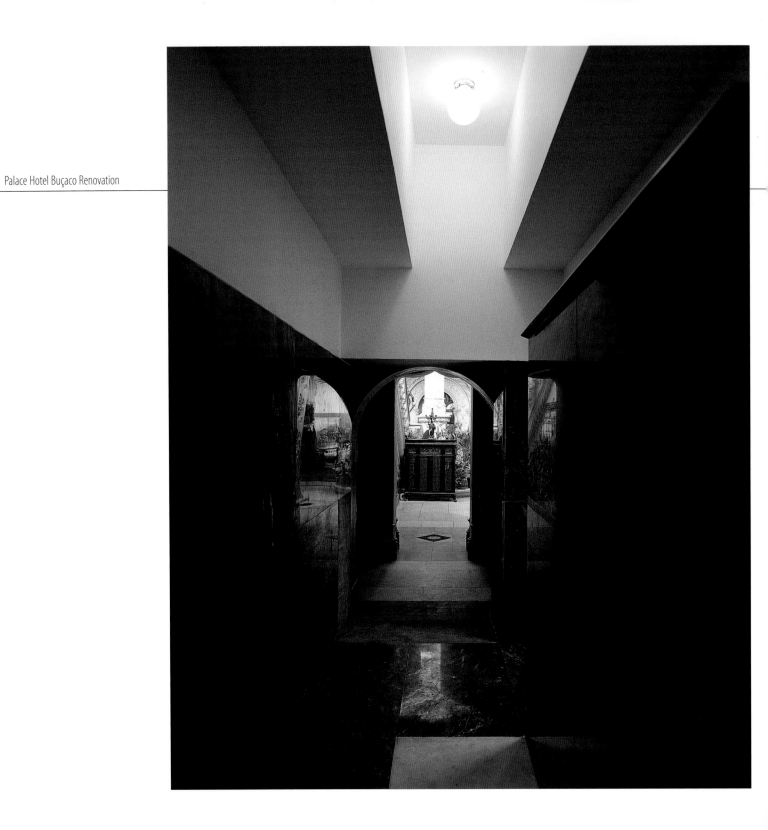

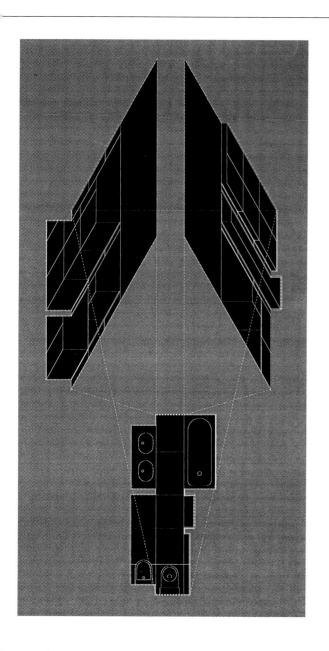

(left, top and middle, and far left)
The formal arrangement of the public
restrooms in the Palacio wing were
dictated by preexisting conditions.
(drawing at left) Axonometric study
of a guest room bath. (left, bottom)
Guest room bath, detail.

Kindertagesstätte

BERLIN, GERMANY

Placed on the northern outskirts of Berlin—in Karow Nord—within a new settlement master-planned by Moore Ruble Yudell, this Kindertagesstätte is among the facilities built by the Senat fur Bauen Wohnunswiesen und Verkehr as the infrastructure complement to the private development of housing units.

The siting takes into account not only the proposed neighborhood, but also the specificity of the program. Two blocks of clear character address the program and the site. The one to the east, facing a pedestrian path, deals with the general entrance and parts of the program that do not fit within the established grid. These parts—protruding and recessed—offer clues to pre-established alignments. The other block, also quite enclosed except for the south façade facing the playground, houses mainly the six group rooms—three on each floor—with ancillary spaces for staff and children close at hand.

Plain red bricks cover both volumes—a given by the client for the public structures—with finishes, hardly fitting within the limited budget, additionally constrained by German preconceptions of rationalization and standardization.

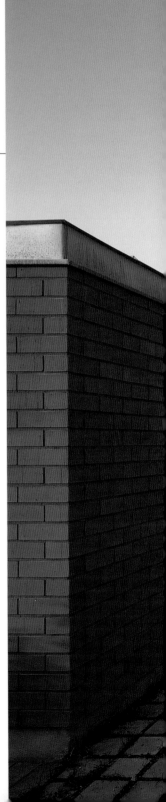

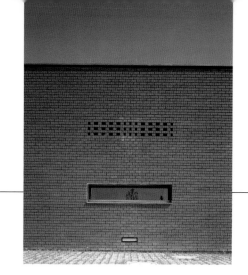

SITE PLAN

(previous spread, left) The Kindertagesstätte (kita) from the south: classrooms are in the left block, the entrance and service area to the right. (previous spread, right) Detail of the glazed link from one volume to the other. (far left) Group rooms, looking from the east. (above left) Detail of window in the service corridor. (left) The kita—sited on a rectangular plot—is in a new housing quarter without any built context except newly constructed housing. The building is positioned on the site to be seen distinctly both from the northern part of the adjacent avenue and from the south.

Kindertagesstätte

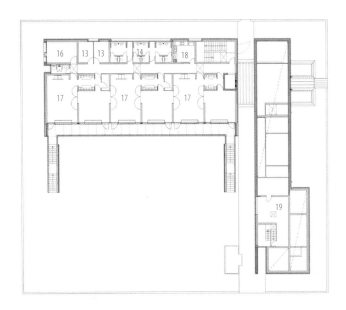

SECOND FLOOR PLAN

18 ANCILLARY KITCHEN
19 GENERAL STORAGE

(above) Group rooms, general view
and (far right) detail of the system
of wooden openings, a further
development of the window system
used first in the Pego house.

FIRST FLOOR PLAN

1   SAGEBOCKWEG
    PEDESTRIAN PATH
2   SERVICE ENTRANCE
3   EMERGENCY EXIT
4   PUBLIC ENTRANCE
5   PRAMS STORAGE
6   MAIN VESTIBULE
7   SUPERVISORS OFFICE
8   KITCHEN
9   KITCHEN STORAGE
10 RESTROOM
11 KITCHEN STAFF ROOM
12 PLANT ROOM
13 STORAGE
14 CHILDREN RESTROOM
15 SICK CHILDREN
16 TUTORS ROOM
17 GROUP ROOM

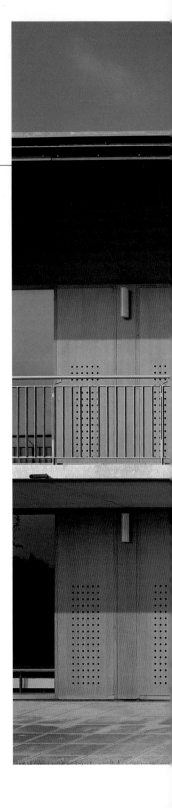

(right) detail at corner of terrace and play wall. (far right) One of the design requirements never fully considered in previous commissions was the thermal behavior of every element in the building. The biggest challenge was the resolution of the design within the DIN's strict rules without losing the elegance and rigor of the detailing.

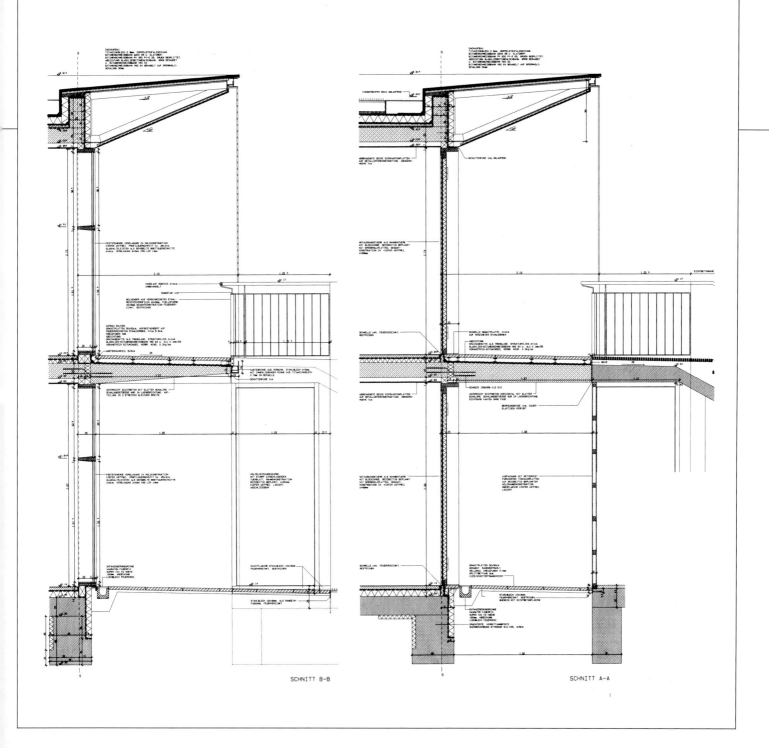

SCHNITT B-B   SCHNITT A-A

In contrast to the large glazed openings on relatively thin wooden frames in the group rooms, from the street the project becomes two almost independent but interconnected monoliths of red brick. (far left, top) West façade, (far left, middle) north façade, and (far left, bottom) south façade, where the main entrance and plant room jut out of the simple volume. (left) Detail, north façade. (following spread, left) North façade, with corresponding sections and elevation, and (following spread, right) south façade, with corresponding sections and elevation. The main public approach to the kita is from the south.

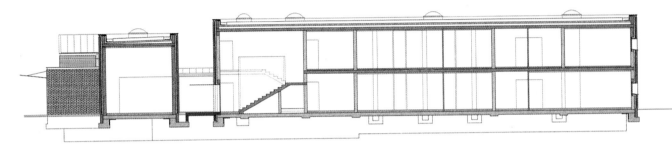

SECTION THROUGH SUPERVISORS OFFICE AND CHILDREN RESTROOMS

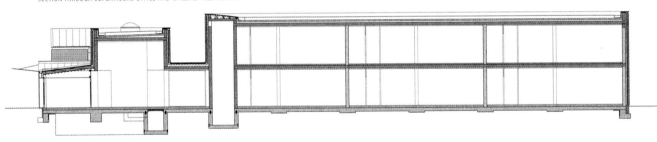

SECTION THROUGH MAIN ENTRANCE AND GROUP ROOMS

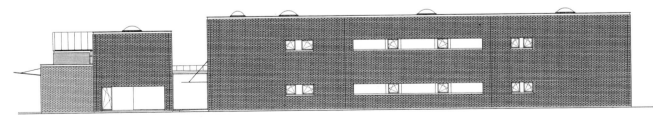

NORTH ELEVATION

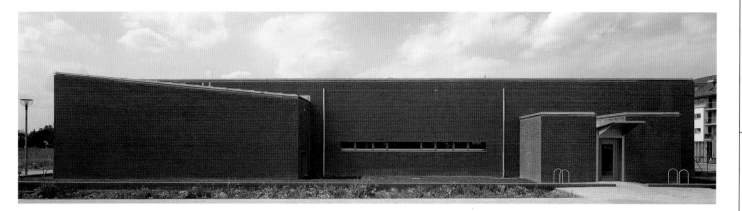

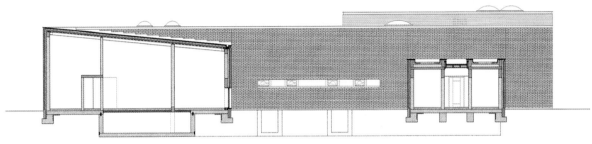

SECTION THROUGH MAIN ENTRANCE AND PLANT ROOM

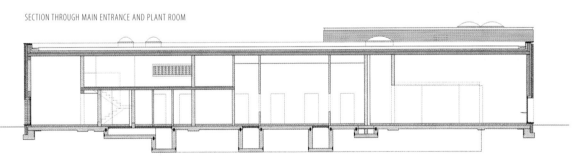

SECTION THROUGH MAIN VESTIBULE AND KITCHEN

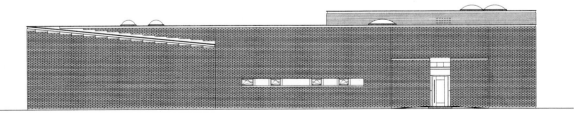

SOTH ELEVATION

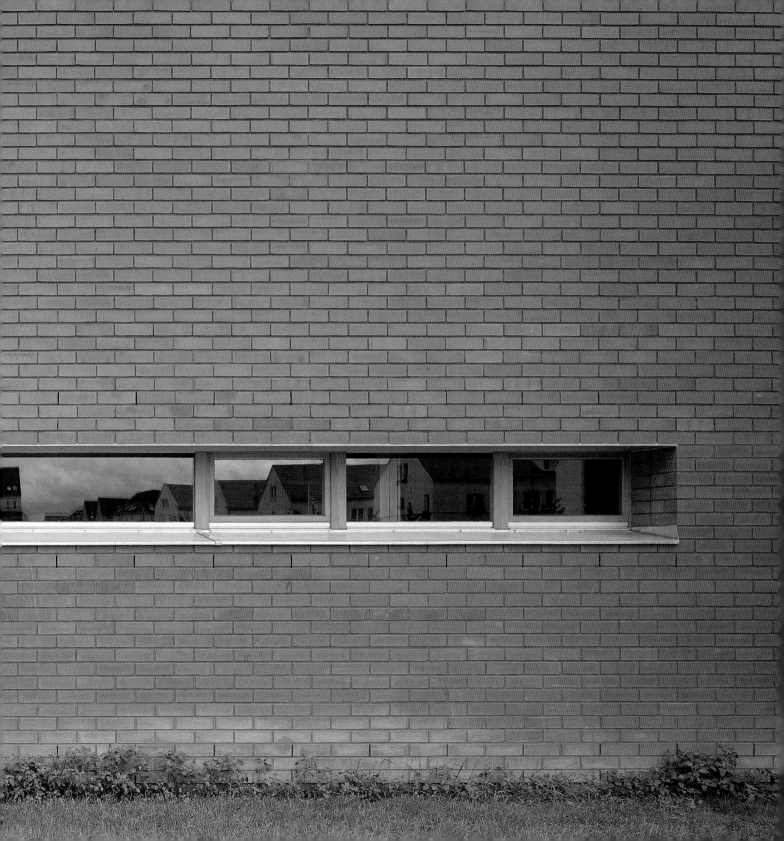

(previous spread) Detail, kitchen window system. (far left) The protruding volume of the main entrance into the kita. (left, top to bottom) Entrance sequence, from street to vestibule.

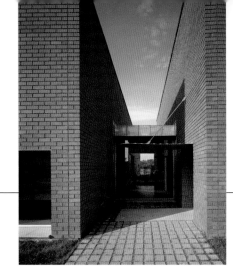

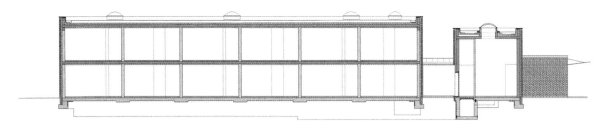

SECTION THROUGH ENTRANCE AND VESTIBULE

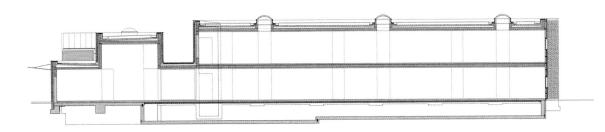

(above) Link between the two built volumes, south with a cast iron overhang door canopy. (far right) Interior view from the passage looking south with the trash storage at the end to the right.

SECTION THROUGH MAIN ENTRANCE AND CORRIDOR

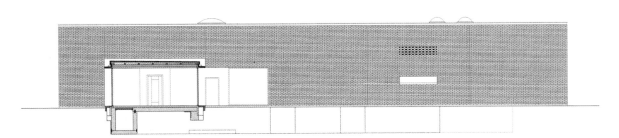

SSECTION THROUGH PASSAGE

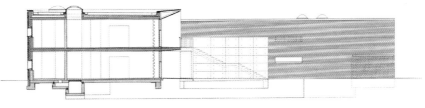

SECTION THROUGH ENTRANCE TO GROUP ROOMS

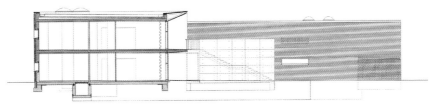

SECTION THROUGH COAT ROOMS IN GROUP ROOMS

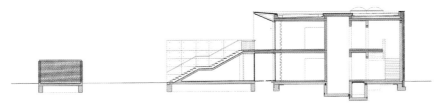

SECTION THROUGH LIFT AND STAIRS

(far left and above) Group room interiors. The sudden budget reduction by the authorities a few weeks before construction was due to start is made evident by, among other things, the reduced height and detailing of the enfilade of sound-proof doors, thereby made inconsistent with the exterior fenestration and the interior and exterior detailing.

(top) Access corridor to group rooms.
(middle) Children's restroom. (bottom)
Children's coat room and storage area.
(far right) Interior of group room
looking into children's changing room.

Loios Convent Renovation and Extension

ARRAIOLOS, PORTUGAL

A place for looking inward and outward, the Loios Convent has through time accommodated similar rituals for different functions. Slightly disguised harmonies, rhythms without a recognizable sequence, faded symmetries, functional clarity in labyrinthine disguise, varying shades of white, all give the convent its tone.

Now, as with previous additions, the primacy of the existing structure is not altered; all its spatial qualities are kept intact. The addition of a new wing enclosing the eastern patio acknowledges not only the implicit formal autonomy of the existing structure, but also its own new rules.

These rules keep the addition consistent with the existing character: simultaneously austere in materials, but rich in form and iconography. An attempt was made to value building forms still available in this country—spontaneous, generous and imbued with the relaxed rigor provided by the sunny planes of the south. If the project has something to say, it should "step forward and be silent."

Loios Convent Renovation and Extension

1   MULTIPURPOSE ROOM
2   SERVICE CORRIDOR
3   DIRECTOR'S APARTMENT
4   STAFF CANTEEN
5   PLANT ROOM
6   LAUNDRY
7   STAFF BEDROOMS
8   VESTIBULE
9   OLD CHAPTER ROOM
10 RECEPTION
11 COVERED CHURCH ANTECHAMBER
12 CHURCH
13 BAR
14 SITTING ROOM
15 PASSAGE
16 MEN'S RESTROOM
17 LADIES' RESTROOM
18 RESTAURANT, OLD WING
19 RESTAURANT, NEW WING
20 KITCHEN
21 ESPLANADE
22 CHANGING ROOM
23 BEDROOMS
24 PATIO
25 EASTERN REFLECTING POOL
26 CLOISTER

SITE PLAN

BASEMENT FLOOR PLAN

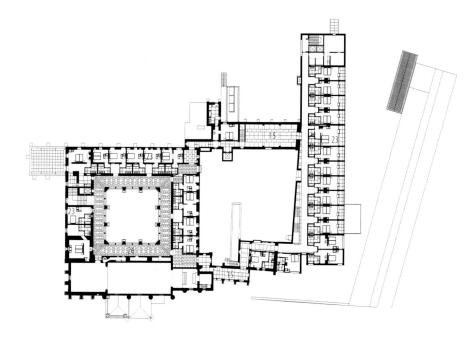

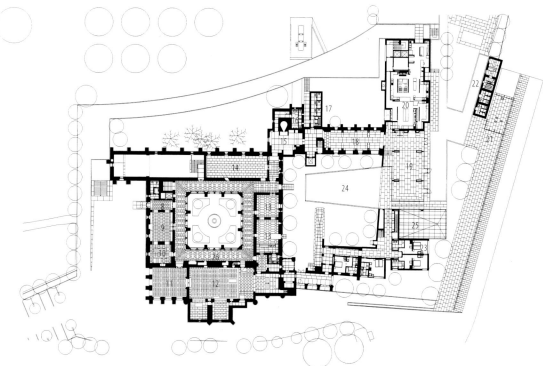

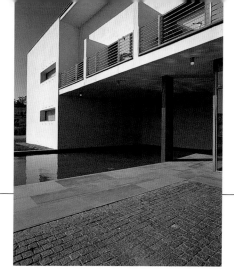

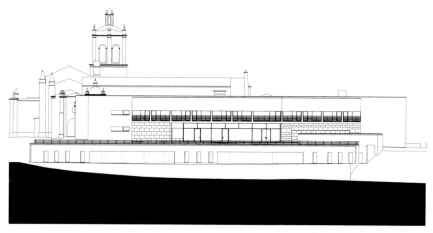

EAST ELEVATION

(opening spread, right) Loios Convent in Arraiolos from the east. (opening spread, left) Detail of passage in the old part of the convent, overlooking the patio. (following double spread) Partial east and south façades. New guest rooms are in the foreground above the reflecting pool; the restaurant is across the patio beyond the reflecting pool, and the kitchen is at the far end. To the left is the link to the old part of the convent. (this page, left) New wing looking south (above) Reflecting pool. (far left) Relationship of the new east wing, with reflecting pool in the foreground, to the terrace and swimming pool beyond.

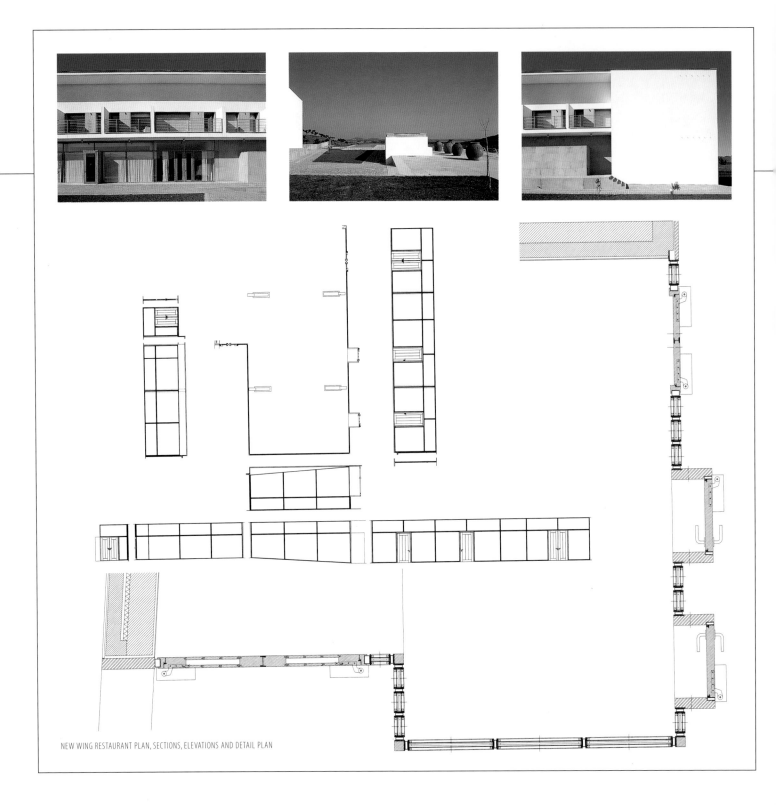

NEW WING RESTAURANT PLAN, SECTIONS, ELEVATIONS AND DETAIL PLAN

(far left) Frontal views of the eastern wing and the swimming pool with a small barn transformed into changing rooms and ventilated pots on the terrace hiding the chimneys from the mechanical equipments below. (left) View of the passage to the patio next to the water basin and restaurant.

(right) Passage from the patio to the terrace, between the reflecting pool and restaurant, looking east. (far right) Patio, looking to the west façade of the new east wing. The main opening at ground level and the recessed opening at the guest room corridor above provide a counterpoint to the openings on the adjacent, existing south façade. The other cooling element is in the right foreground.

SOUTH ELEVATION (BOTTOM) AND SECTION TROUGH SITTING ROOM, PATIO AND NEW WING RESTAURANT LOOKING NORTH (TOP)

NORTH ELEVATION (BOTTOM) AND SECTION TROUGH PASSAGE AND NEW AND OLD WING RESTAURANT LOOKING SOUTH (TOP)

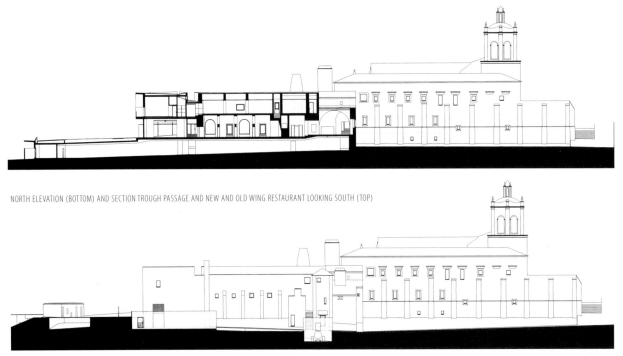

(far left) The new wing of the convent is sited next to the old agricultural structures extending into the north part of the complex. It is eminently modern in terms of structure, language and materials, and this modernity is balanced by a series of "unconscious" rules drawn from the countryside and from the exquisite internal geometrical relationships drawn from the hotel particulier type. (left) The patio, looking northeast.

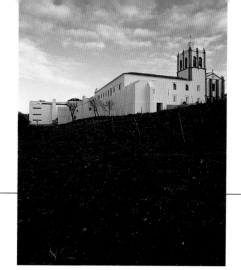

WEST ELEVATION (TOP) AND SECTIONS TROUGH PATIO (BOTTOM LEFT) AND CONVENT (BOTTOM RIGHT) LOOKING EAST

(far left) Overall view from the north-west shows the gradual progression of service elements and additions toward the northeast portion of the convent. (Above) The main entrance is on the west façade, with service access through the north façade. (left) Detail of a series of additions on the north: the old kitchen, the director's quarters, and the new kitchen and service area.

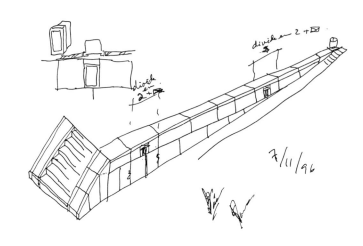

7/11/96

(right, top to bottom) Main entrance sequence. (far right) Due to the client's requirements, the cloister had to be enclosed. The initial attitude was purer; the final result, given the capabilities of the local glass industry, is a compromise.

The existing chapel has merely been cleaned and furnished with simple stools and tables, handcrafted with care by cabinetmakers still at work in the north of the country.

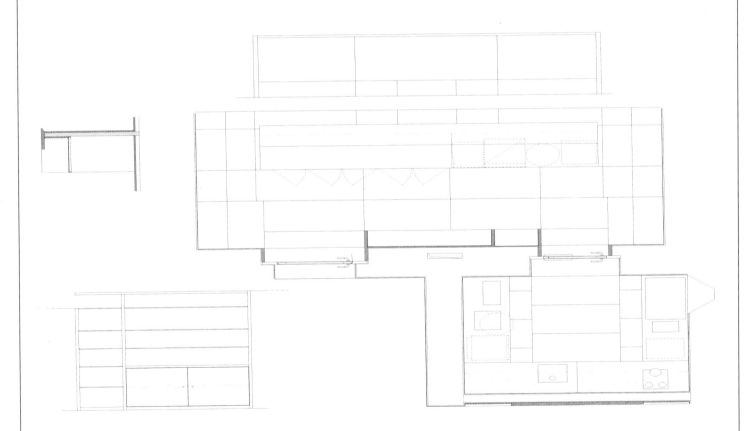

BAR PLAN, ELEVATION AND SECTION

The lower-level public area involved substantial intervention kept quiet in attitude so that what was existing remains serene amid the necessary garb of technology.

(far left) The former kitchen was kept intact, now part of the labyrinthine system of corridors. (left, top) A nun overlooks the passage to the upper levels. (left, middle and bottom) Women's restroom.

(right, bottom and far right) A former cow shed, part of the old convent, now houses a portion of the restaurant, whose kitchen is in the new east wing. (right, top and middle) The dividing wall separating the kitchen from the new part of the restaurant.

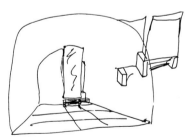

eo dem.

(far left) Upstairs corridor. The blue signals structural "accidents." (left, top and bottom) The back of the former oven along the path to the men's restroom on the ground floor. (middle) Detail of narrow, low passage on the upper level. (following spread, left to right) Corridor, new wing. A recessed, low window overlooking the patio is complemented by a wide, tall window at the end of the corridor overlooking the town of Arraiolos and the fantastic remains of its small castle. (second spread, left to right) The new cells are wide open to the countryside, as counterpoint to the solid frugality of closets in the outer walls of the old cells.

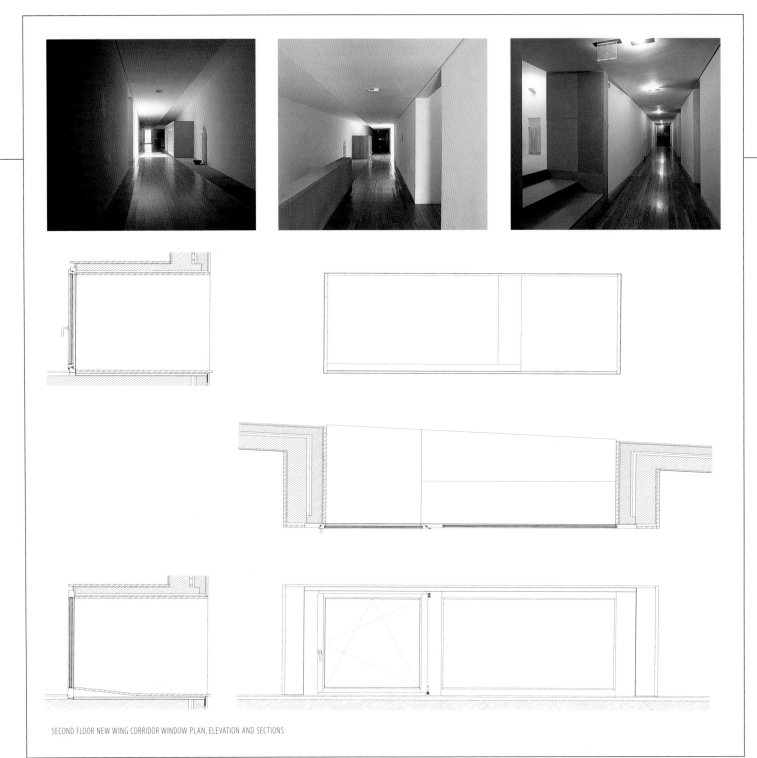

SECOND FLOOR NEW WING CORRIDOR WINDOW PLAN, ELEVATION AND SECTIONS

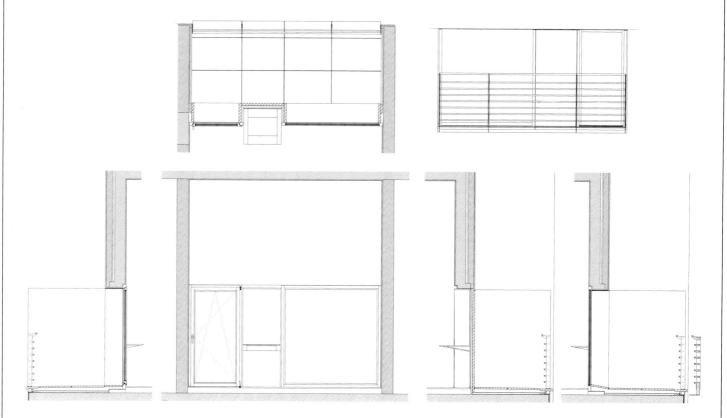

SECOND FLOOR NEW WING BEDROOM TYPICAL BALCONY PLAN, ELEVATION AND SECTIONS

Tombstones, V.N. Monsarros

VILA NOVA DE MONSARROS, PORTUGAL

These stones belong to the private patrimony of affections; not, perhaps, to architecture, as in "the tomb and the monument." In the local cemetery—poor and almost chaotic, like all cemeteries in this part of the countryside—are laid to rest a couple and their two sons, simple and warm people.

Each of the granite slabs, with stainless steel encrustation, sits on simple, cubic granite foundations—leaving the earth otherwise untouched. The steel is meant as a counterpoint to the roughness of the stone; just as the people lying beneath were gentle but hearty fighters on sterile soil.

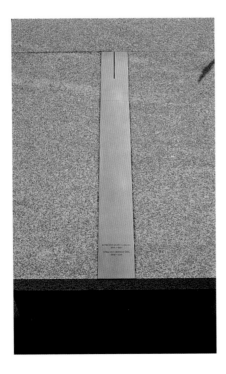

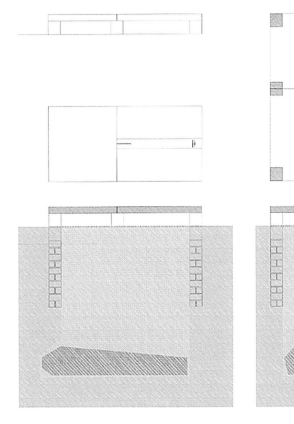

TOMBS PLAN, ELEVATION AND SECTIONS

Appendix ▶

HOUSE IN CASCAIS II   Cascais, Portugal

SECOND FLOOR PLAN   FIRST FLOOR PLAN

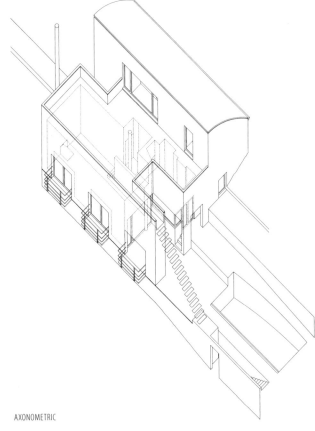

AXONOMETRIC

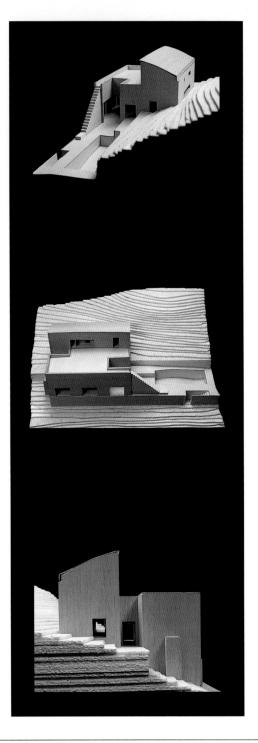

HOUSE IN LUSO   Luso, Portugal

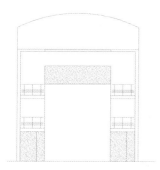

WEST ELEVATION

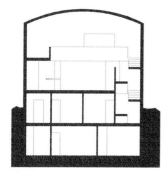

SECTION LOOKING EAST

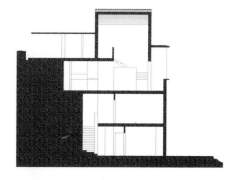

SECTION LOOKING SOUTH

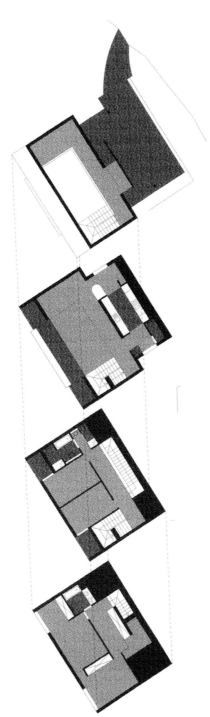

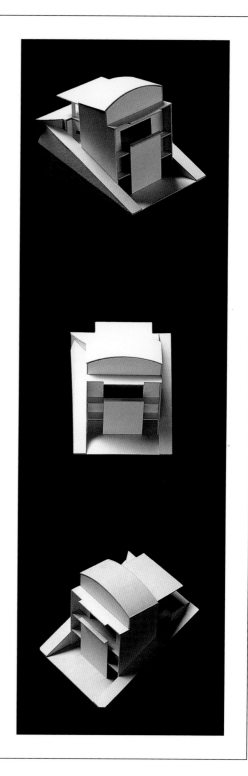

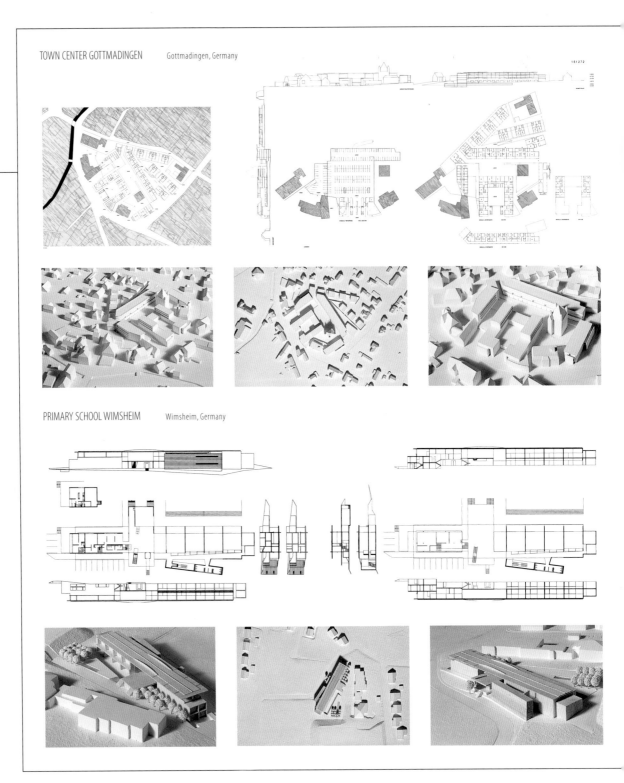

TOWN CENTER GOTTMADINGEN   Gottmadingen, Germany

PRIMARY SCHOOL WIMSHEIM   Wimsheim, Germany

REICHSTAG BERLIN   Berlin, Germany

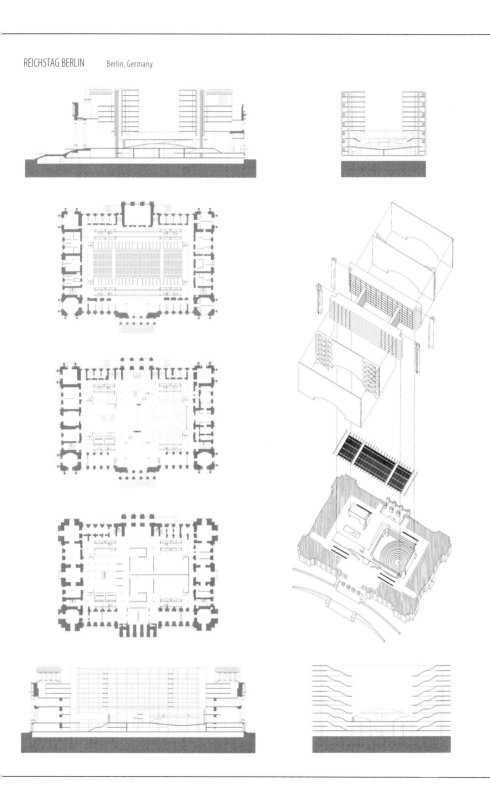

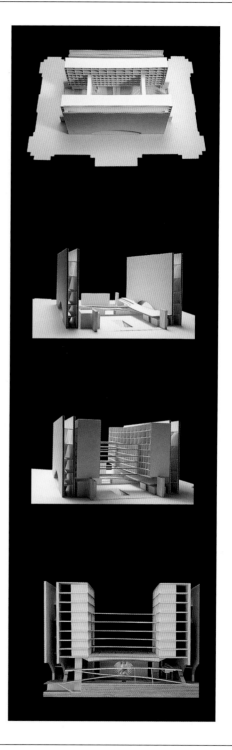

MUSEUM DER BILDENDEN KÜNSTE Leipzig, Germany

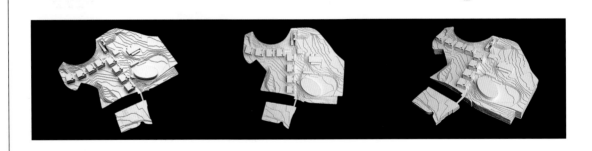

ST. AFRA GRAMMAR SCHOOL Meissen, Germany

BIS, BANK FOR INTERNATIONAL SETTLEMENTS Basel, Switzerland

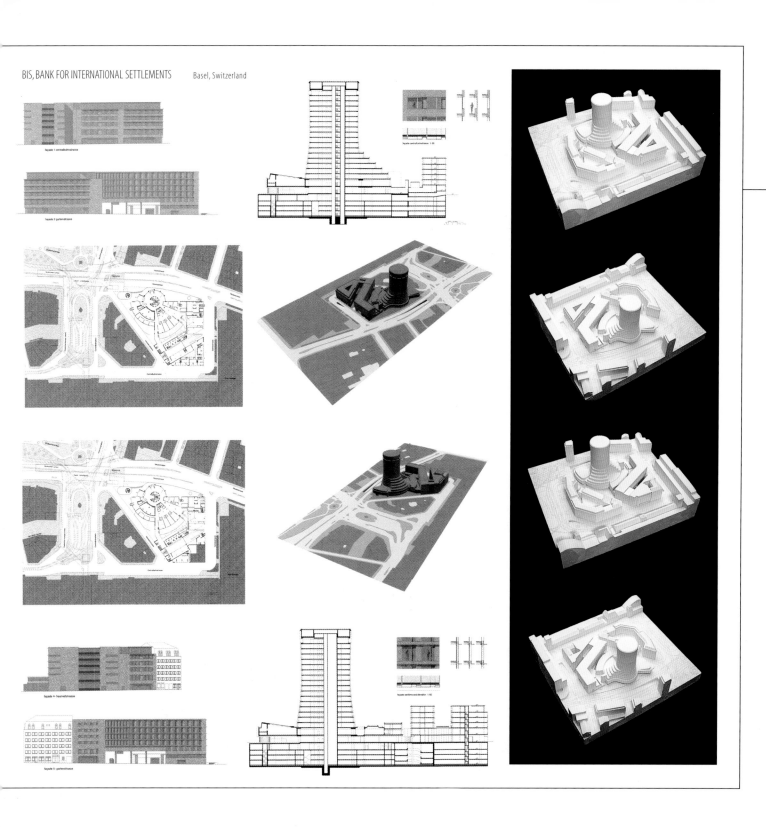

ALFRIED KRUPP HAUS, RESEARCH CENTER   Greifswald, Germany

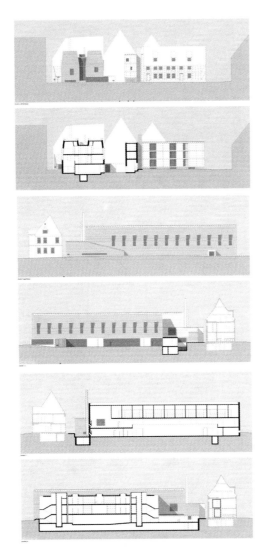

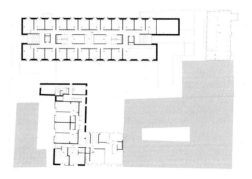

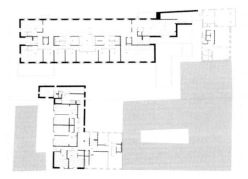

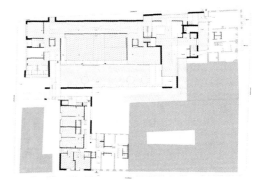

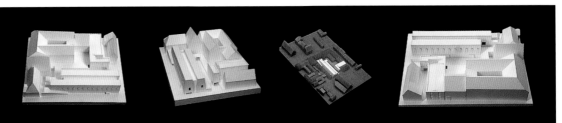

MACHADO DE CASTRO NACIONAL MUSEUM   Coimbra, Portugal

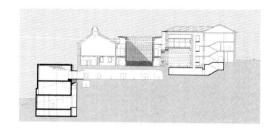

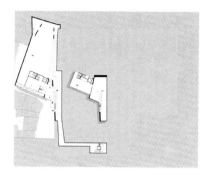

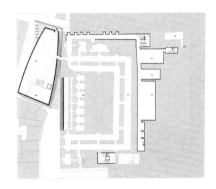

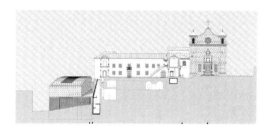

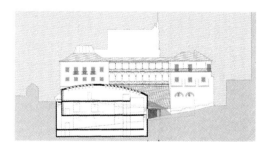

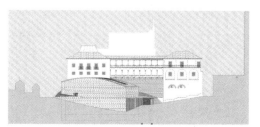

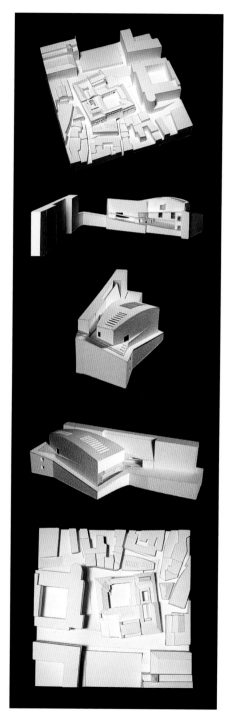

List of Works and Credits

HOUSE IN PEGO
1994, Pego, Portugal
Client: António Pimenta
Architect: José Paulo dos Santos
Collaborator: António José Teixeira
Photographer: Luis Ferreira Alves

TOURIST OFFICE REFURBISHMENT
1985-1987, Luso, Portugal
Architect: José Paulo dos Santos
Collaborators: Jorge Nuno Monteiro, António José Teixeira
Builder: Armando Fachada
Photographer: Luis Ferreira Alves

AUTOPSY ROOM AND MORGUE
1986-1988, Lisbon, Portugal,
Architect: José Paulo dos Santos
Collaborators: Jorge Nuno Monteiro, António José Teixeira
Structures: José Adriano
Electricity: Rodrigues Gomes
Air Conditioning: Costa Pereira
Builder: ENVAF
Photographer: Luis Ferreira Alves

PALACE HOTEL BUÇACO RENOVATION
1987-1991, Buçaco, Portugal
Architect: José Paulo dos Santos
Collaborator: António José Teixeira
Structures: Teles de Oliveira
Electrical and Security: Rodrigues Gomes
Air conditioning: Afonso Mira
Water and Sewage: Humberto Vieira
General Contractor: Ventura e Pires, Coimbra
Water and Electricity Contractor: F. de Oliveira , Coimbra
Air Conditioning Contractor: Electroclima, Coimbra
Lifts Contractor: Otis, Coimbra
Security Contractor: Securitas, Coimbra
Office Collaborators: António José Teixeira, Christian Gaenshirt, Rui Castro, Anne Wermeille
Photographer: Luis Ferreira Alves

KINDERTAGESSTÄTTE
1996-1999,Berlin, Germany
Awarded 1998 architekturpreis des Bund Deutscher Architekten,Berlin
Architecture: José Paulo dos Santos and Barbara Hoidn
Collaboration: Oliver Ulmer, António José Teixeira
Bauleiter: Manfred Schurr
Engineers: Emch & Berger
Landscape: Schmitz & Wolny
Client: Senat Fur Bauen Wohnungswiesen Und Verkehr
Photographer: Christian Richters

LOIOS CONVENT RENOVATION AND EXTENSION
1993-1999, Arraiolos, Portugal
Client: ENATUR
Architect: José Paulo dos Santos
Interiors: Cristina Guedes and José Paulo dos Santos
Structures: ETEC
Water and Sewage: ETEC
Electrical and Security: Rodrigues Gomes
Air Conditioning: Rodrigues Gomes
Quantity Surveyor: N Bertini
Photographer: Luis Ferreira Alves

TOMBSTONES, V.N. MONSARROS
1995, Vila Nova de Monsarros, Portugal
Architect: José Paulo dos Santos
Photographer: Luis Ferreira Alves

HOUSE IN CASCAIS II
1991, Cascais, Portugal
Client: Luis Gonçalves
Architect: José Paulo dos Santos
Collaborators: António José Teixeira, Christian Gaenshirt
Model Photos: Arménio Teixeira

HOUSE IN LUSO
1994, Luso, Portugal
Client: J R Santos
Architect: José Paulo dos Santos
Collaborator: António José Teixeira
Model Photos: Arménio Teixeira

TOWN CENTER GOTTMADINGEN/COMPETITION

1996, Gottmadingen, Germany

Architect: José Paulo dos Santos

Collaborators: Oliver Ulmer, António José Teixeira

Model Photos: José Paulo dos Santos archives

PRIMARY SCHOOL WIMSHEIM/COMPETITION

1997, Wimsheim, Germany

Architect: José Paulo dos Santos

Collaborators: Oliver Ulmer, António José Teixeira

Model Photos: José Paulo dos Santos archives

REICHSTAG BERLIN/COMPETITION

1992, Berlin, Germany

Client: Bundes Baudirektion

Architect: José Paulo dos Santos and Barbara Hoidn

Collaborators: António José Teixeira, Rui Castro

Model Photos: José Paulo dos Santos archives

MUSEUM DER BILDENDEN KÜNSTE/COMPETITION

1997, Leipzig, Germany

Architect: José Paulo dos Santos

Collaborators: Oliver Ulmer, António José Teixeira

Model Photos: José Paulo dos Santos archives

ST. AFRA GRAMMAR SCHOOL/COMPETITION

1997, Meissen, Germany

Architect: José Paulo dos Santos

Collaborators: Oliver Ulmer, António José Teixeira

Client: St. Afra Grammar School

Model Photos: Arménio Teixeira

BIS, BANK FOR INTERNATIONAL SETTLEMENTS EXTENSION/INVITED COMPETITION

1998, Basle, Switzerland

Architect: José Paulo dos Santos

Collaborators: Oliver Ulmer, António José Teixeira

Model Photos: Arménio Teixeira

ALFRIED KRUPP HAUS, RESEARCH CENTER INVITED/COMPETITION

1999, Greifswald ,Germany

Architect: José Paulo dos Santos

Collaborators: Oliver Ulmer, António José Teixeira

Client: Alfried Krupp von Bohlen und Halbach - Stiftung

Model Photos: Arménio Teixeira

MACHADO DE CASTRO, NATIONAL MUSEUM CLOSED/COMPETITION

1999, Coimbra, Portugal

Architect: José Paulo dos Santos

Collaborators: Oliver Ulmer, António José Teixeira

Model Photos: Arménio Teixeira

JOSE PAULO DOS SANTOS OFFICE COLLABORATORS:
1984—2000

José Fernando Gonçalves

Alfredo Vilarinho

António José Teixeira

Christian Gaenshirt

Anne Wermeille

Rui Castro

Paulo Pinto

Andrea Krupski

Oliver Ulmer

Alberto Laje

Karl-Eugen Maute

Joahnnes Fritsch

Rui Neto

(Above from left to right) Anne Wermeille, José Paulo dos Santos and António José Teixeira at José Paulo dos Santos' offices in Porto.

ACKNOWLEDGMENTS

the various offices that had me as an apprentice

the various friends and colleagues in architecture

both abroad and at home

my office collaborators along the years

Luis Ferreira Alves for his stillness grasp of life and enthusiastic storytelling

Gerrit Confurius for discerning about the years of practice

Oscar Riera Ojeda for his care towards my work and patience towards me.

my father